THE PRINCESS OF CASTRO STREET

Short Stories From Fast Times

The Plunge to Power in a Shallow Pool

HRH LEE MENTLEY

ACKNOWLEDGEMENTS

A Gypsy Told Me
Remember
The Fog Is Weird
&
The Moon Is Your Friend.

DEDICATED TO MY SWEETHEART, JUSTIN

EDITORS

Ken Dickmann, Jim Campbell. Edward Vilga, Robert Croonquist, Pérez
I Thank & Apologize to all of you for writing a book that belongs
in a plain brown wrapper...!

Mother Sarah Bassi & Bassi Sisters along with Uncle Nicky, Gogo, Todd Singerman, Larry Cronen, Pérez, Michael Cuomo, Shauna Hankoff, Pamela Goodlow Green, Alex Green, Andy Batioff, Les Plush, Iory Allison, Jim Campbell, Joseph Suarez, Sam Bullock, Michael Shain, Ken Dickmann, Martin Worman, Robert Croonquist, Demetrie Kabbaz, Dolores Deluce, Danny Nicoletta, Tommy Kohl, Mark Thompson, Stuart Timmons, Jimmy Coker, Adrian Craig, Glenn Stroud, John Warren, John Wahl, Robert Oppel, Janice Roland, Jane Gottlieb, Anna Powell, Sheila Doyle, Maggie Lind, Lady Dianna, Fred Bradford, Glenne McElhinney, Nathan Kalama, Bobby Yoder, Justin Lier, Sandra Rivkin, The Cockettes, The Angeles of Light, Mink Stole, Divine, Edward Vilga, Paul Hardman, and Harvey Milk.

Thanks for the ears, equipment, inspiration, edits and encouragement...!

Matter & Energy
Nucleolus Cell
Center of Eternity
Religions Fell

Mother Sarah Bassi Mentley
Hart Smith Rodriguez.
Family Photographer.

Cover photo: "Always Two Sides To A Pancake" at the Gallery Theatre in the Secret Cinema, starring Mink Stole and Lee Mentley, 1972. Photographer unknown. Back cover: top photo by Daniel Nicoletta. Painting and photograph by Jim Campbell.
Cover & Book Design: Tim Lewis

Facebook.com/HRHLeeMentley
Copyright Lee Mentley 2016

TABLE OF CONTENTS

"I'm rather breathless from gasping after reading the introduction...,
after I pick up a supply of oxygen no doubt I'll swim through!"
— Les Plush

PROLOGUE

The Hula Palace

In the Beginning We Were Truly Gay.
How did we get the name, "The Hula Palace?"

M any of the homes in Castro Village had titles. It was time for us to join in the fun. There was the Upper Market Street Gallery, where you could usually find the chanteuse diva Sylvester sprawled across the grand piano in thirties femme fatale drag, gardenias in her hair straight from swap meets and the ghetto of La La Land.

There were the homes of Flo Airways, Cafe Ole, Nocturnal Dreams, Secret Cinema, Magdalena Montezuma's Mansion with Paola Del Vecchio, Candy Ass plus Mother and Baby, Lena the

Leopard Lady, and Sally Swell, The Film Madness Club, Madd Helen's Emporium, and La Casa Chica. There was Joe Morocco and Janice Sukaitis at The Ranch. The Bourgeois Palace, The Ritz Place, The Ho Chi Minh Palace, Jano's Salon, the Marquee's Maison Vingt-Neuf, Kaliflower Commune, The Pink Palace, Chatty Cathy's House, Aunty Emm's and Mona's Hideaway, and Hunga

Hula Palace, Painting by Jim Campbell,
Photo by Lee Mentley

Dunga House among many more interesting haunts.

And there was Glitter's Castle, where I lived for short stints with sculptor Bobby Burnside and Goldie Glitters, star of Tricia's Wedding, of the Cockette's fame. We breakfasted with her new best friend the awesome Divine, until there was this horrible reoccurring infestation of crabs and a hitchhiker with fleas from blowing the dog. But I digress ...

One afternoon, I, The Princess "ELA Lee," aka "Lee Lee," aka "Master Bastard" was strolling with Iory Allison aka the "Tibetan Princess," aka "Starr," aka "Sissy," and "Bitch". We had just come from seeing a bizarre satire on a dead musician from the old world at a matinee in The Cannery. I think it was The Music Lovers, about a Russian queer composer, but it made me dizzy and I threw up in the gutter!

We trolleyed up Market and walked through Castro Village to 19th Street. We walked up the long stairs to more dizziness. As the door opened we could hear THE GURLLLS! Arguing in the front salon, there was The Handsome Prince, Cowboy Robert Kirk, aka Cirby. He was clamoring, "I don't want to call my home 'The Blue Swan Hotel.' This is a man's house. It's 'The Five Star Dude Ranch.'"

We walked down the hall and peaked in at demure Etta aka "Leslie Plush," "Les," "Linda Carne," "ErLinda" and/or "Etta Linda." Etta was listening to Cirby, Rachael, and Ms. Blue going at it. This was the boy/girl menagerie I called "roommates."

The Tibetan Princess demanded, "What's all the fuss about?"

Girllls...?

GURLLLS...!

ATTENTION...!

GIRLLLS...!

Each of us shared with our flock why we wanted a different name for our lovely Victorian flat.

Cirby wanted it to be a real man's man name, a home on the range kind of thing. "Do something Iory before I throw up...again!" Then Starr's eyes sparkled. His eyebrows raised and lowered. She announced, "Get over it Girllls, wagging his finger at Cirby, "You, too, Dale Evans—Dude Ranch indeed!" Starr continued, "Get a-grip ladies! This is just a Hula Palace and you're all just a bunch of lovely little Hula Maidens!"

Etta and I screamed, "Yes....! Yes....!" We knew that was it! This was The Hula Palace! We were the Matson Line Girls! And no one could deny it. I mean look at the hundreds of Aloha shirts both Etta and I had, and the fifty or sixty or so muumuus we had in our closets as well. It was perfect. The Tibetan bitch had totally nailed it.

We would have to have a debut, a celebration, a prom, a luau, a coming out party be-fitting Gay Hawaiian Faux Royaltie, paper leis and all. We knew from the inside out only drag could save the world.

We planned our first Hula Palace Salon to correspond with the arrival of winter solstice and the comet Kohoutek. We sang, we danced, we shared our art!

Suddenly, before we knew it, museum directors were attending our salons. Something was happening.

INTRODUCTION

HRH POINT OF VIEW

"The Princess of Castro Street"

Short Stories from Fast Times is a collection of selected episodes, essays and letters.

Subtitles: "The Plunge to Power in a Shallow Pool"

Like all good stories, let's start at the beginning...,

When I was a little gurl, I wanted to grow up and become a beatnik...,

Perhaps more accurately, this is a collection of fast images, three very silly and three political, horrid—all fleeting intentions of deranged minds.

These stories are solely from my own experience and told from multiple inner perspectives. They are shards—discovered in a house of broken mirrors—reflecting personal images of a unique time in my life.

These are my personal observations from my front row seat at what could be called "The Gay Games of the 1970s": the Hula Palace Salon and San Francisco Politics. During a time of sexual revolution, I witnessed the birth of San Francisco's Gay Movement in the Castro. The stories within are a reflection

Little Lorraine, Erie PA. Photo by Mommy

6

of my point of view of that process, including the point of view of my alter ego HRH The Princess, a conversation from my future with my past.

Speaking of time, with few exceptions, events in these stories did not all happen in the chronological order I recall. Everything written here is accompanied by the term "allegedly".

In the same way some characters have been morphed into composites.

Given the perpetual motion and dramatic impossibilities that mix the genders in real life, even pronouns are in flux. The words "Girl," "Gurl," "Grrrr" "She" or "Her" might pertain to the same individual regardless of traditional concepts of gender; even the vowels can change their rhythm and repetitions that imply some notion with range and tone of voice, as in Guurrrlll, or Sheeeee, we make believe we are male and female, quantum-entangled, flesh and blood paper dolls, stretched out across the multiverse of time and sound.

It's that kind of time, that kind of tale...

* * *

What is freedom...?

I often hear how we are a free people, only to be scolded for saying or doing something no one wants to hear or see. "Shut Up Gurl".

So I will apologize now for not being the nice and good person friends and family want me to be.

How can you be free when you are told to use a letter rather than a word? The "N word," the "C word," the "F word, the "T word?"

If you are that frail—stay home! To quote Her Royal Highness Mz. Penny Arcade, this is "The Tyranny of Fragility."

The Princess of Castro Street is not meant to be an intellectual history of the secular humanistic homosexual gay movement, as Mr. Randy Shilts presented in his so-called definitive book, The Mayor of Castro Street.

Shilts claims to have chronicled the life and times of Harvey Milk, who in the White Picket Fence World is seen as the first openly homosexual elected to public office in San Francisco's recorded history. Shilts was sadly lost in a world of "Politically Correct" hero worship. His work is betrayed by a notion of glamor that's more or less entirely veiled. He sees the world through a shroud of money and power. He had no idea who Harvey Milk the artist was

7

or how change actually occurred in The Castro. For example, I find it deeply significant that the 330 Grove Pride Foundation Gay Community Center—a landmark that is vital to an understanding of the time—and hallmarked in Harvey Milk's 'HOPE' speech is never mentioned in Shilts' or other "definitive" histories written about the period. Why?

Milk was Our Mayor; I was a Princess. We lived as make-believe royalty. This was a very different world. We lived in an exotic, erotic dream of universal archetypes colliding on the world stage. "Truth" as in the 'First World' was an illusion to comfort the weak and gullible who wanted desperately to be normal. We did not want to be normal.

In Shilts' book, he presents a version of what the San Francisco militant "Politically Correct," or the "Gayourgeoisie" as I call the gay bourgeoisie, wanted to be reality. I was not part of this because I was not, and still am not "Politically Correct." I'll call you a fag hag or a shemale a "shemale" if she or he is and wants to be free to be who she is.

Shilts presents a picture void of any real life, free from any of the juicy, gritty dirt we lived through daily. Although he does relate a few nasty details about the San Francisco Police Department, he fails the people who created and hosted the dance. He caters to the ones who eventually claimed it as their own. These are the same people who would still be in the closet today if we, "The Truly Gay," had not taken the risks for them in the 70s. It's an unacknowledged legacy, creating a generation that now thinks "we are safe" because they cannot see past their illusion of being "normal" and just like everyone else behind their "white picket fence."

* * * * *

It was a time of glorious conflict and shimmering change. It was a time when gurlish "Vamp" was in vogue and there was nostalgia for the early 1900s, the Roaring New York 20s, the 30s, Cabaret Society, Glamorized 40s Pin-Up Girls, 50s Poodle Skirts, Cole Porter, Loretta Young, Jeanette McDonald, Piaf, Gore Vidal, the not-quite-yet-over-with 1960s, the wild beasts of the 18th century—essentially all interesting times past, present and future as they related to sexual allure—with enough drugs to see our gray cells burst against bug lights!

Everyone wanted to be "Fashionably Festive" by day and pantheistic rogues by night—or visa versa. We were really big on visa versa: boys being gurls, girls being boys, the guilty rich being poor, and the poor feigning wealth. The artists who passed through the Hula Palace in San Francisco in the 1970s were living in nontraditional family units in haunted Victorian flats and storefronts in what had been an Irish Catholic working class neighborhood that eventually became known as The Castro. It was to become a refuge for all those who were different.

Artists had moved to The Castro to escape the bad drugs and political violence of the Haight Ashbury of the late 1960s and the dullness of mainstream thought. They were, and are, extraordinarily talented and magical people, who the world should know as the creators of a frighteningly odd yet warm life in the mist of the cold San Francisco fog of reality. How they lived, how much fun was had, and how much love was in this gritty, glittering time was truly remarkable. This unique reality was about to burst onto the world stage.

Much of what you see today in clothing design, jewelry, graphics and other art forms were given new perspectives by this zany movement of intense creative angels who twisted and reused everything they could find in a new way. The range of artists touched by this time and place is staggering: Sandra Bernhard, Bette Midler, Robin Williams, The Pointer Sisters, Cher, Sylvester, Annie Leibovitz, Peter Minton, John Waters, Mink Stole, and the impact of the independent aberration of Divine, Robert Mapplethorpe, The Village People personifying gay clones, Queen, k.d. lang, Donna Summer, Bowie, Annie Lennox, the heartfelt passion of Harvey Fierstein, Lily Tomlin, Patrick Cowley and Ellen Degeneres. In diverse ways, they are all children basking in the insanity created by the offbeat nostalgia that gave the past twisted new meanings by the infamous gender-fuck theatrical troupe, The Cockettes, with Sylvester and Angels of Light in their glittered beards and spiritual gurlish attitudes.

We were thrilled by the grand arrival of monstrous, magnificent artists from strange and unusual places like Baltimore. America's newest and most exciting film maker, John Waters, emerged with his stars—Divine, Mink Stole, Edie "The Egg Lady, Edith Massey" and Divine's incredible make-up artist Van Sinclair Smith. I have never enjoyed anything in theater as much as I have enjoyed the talents of Divine. Divine made us all grow up instantly. He showed us what it was to play with reality. Life was Divine. She turned us mere gurls into divas and she loved my mother Sarah who she more or less played in Pink Flamingoes without even knowing she had nailed my mom's character onscreen.

And somehow all of this leads to the present, with men in pastel business suits, to media-savvy women powerfully attired like Rachel Maddow, or to the color-coordinated Anderson Cooper or Don Lemon floating openly above the glass ceiling.

* * * * *

Years later on the remote island of Kaua'i, a highlight of this beautiful blue planet, I asked myself, "If I don't write my stories down, who will remember the truly gay joy?"

Who recalls the glittered beards worn by strange sisters purchased from the crafts counter at Cliff's Variety on Castro Street? Who does know that what eventually became Glitter Rock and Disco had emerged in great part from this village of mystical artists? Or that this was a time when Punk Rock left London, traveled through New York City, arrived in San Francisco, and left as New Wave with Winston Tong, Tuxedomoon, The Mutants & Noh Mercy?

If it weren't for the flamboyance of Hibiscus emerging every Easter Sunday as Jesus parading down through The Castro, from the top of the hill as a pageant unto himself, or the radical gender-fuck drag queens doing their antics in the streets with their multi-pierced ears and brightly colored hair and clothing, there couldn't be "Regular Guys" feeling stable and normal in haute couture and diamond and pearl earrings bouncing off the walls to Amy Winehouse and Lady Gaga today.

* * * * *

Who were we…? What were we…?

We were the Mad Hatters! We were baby gods on soiled streets creating new universes! We were Alice in our own Wonderlands. Like Isadora Duncan, we were dancers at the end of time.

What became known as "The Gay Movement" came later, after the excitement of the artists in The Castro.

When its artists became popular in the media, everyone wanted to be seen on Castro Street. Our Mad Hatter characters were winding their way into the daily papers. All the queens had gossip columnist Herb Caen's phone number inked on their wrists and would kill to be mentioned in his column. It had become THE Hot place to be and, unfortunately, as is the case, this meant it was getting to be time for the people who'd made it chic to be told to leave. This time by the Gayourgeoisie who were more interested in profit than the open door we had created for them filled with human rights and joy!

As a result of all the publicity, visibility and media spin, pretty soon we were attacked by bored, intolerant homophobic young thugs from the South

Bay and the Mission, usually the sons of police officers and closeted sissies from archaic religious traditions. They would joyride through the recently revealed "gay ghetto." We were literally beaten in the streets for being too fashionable.

Then, one holiday weekend, Labor Day I believe, or maybe not, the San Francisco police came into the loosely formed community and attempted to close us down at Andy's Donuts on Castro Street, a 24-hour haunt of the emerging gay community. They arrested several fairies that were fluttering about on the street.

That was the moment when one exuberant New York artist, Harvey Milk, came to the rescue and became our neighborhood hero. Milk was an accomplished and polished performer with a heart of gold. He seized the moment and the spotlight and the SFPD backed down. We had the first ever Gay/Police conference. Later, when Anita Bryant a right wing Christian hack attacked us from Florida, Milk brought The Castro onto the world stage. He

Hula Palace Salon. Photo by Lee Mentley

opened our collective closet doors so wide they will never close again. We all owe him our right hand or whichever hand you use!

The politics that seeped into our reality was both exciting and repulsive. There was a lot of power to be had. There were many unnecessary, nasty political fights. Even so, Harvey knew how to bring all the various diverse factions together. We had our noble leader.

His campaign slogan was "Harvey Milk Verses the Machine" but the Gay-ourgeoisie sycophants were everywhere, already creating a new machine of their own. Danger lie ahead.

Then in an instant, just as quickly, we had our bloodied martyr. Unfortunately, there has been no one to replace him and The Castro has been lost to profit mongers.

* * * * *

It was no secret that after George Moscone was elected Mayor and Harvey Milk elected Supervisor, the power structure of San Francisco changed radically. The jealous Old Guard wasn't happy.

The Good Old Boys in the San Francisco Police Department had to dance to a new tune, played by the new socially liberal mayor in City Hall. Newly elected Mayor Moscone had put a stop to the Good Old Boy Machine all over town—or so he thought.

No one could deny the city was changing. The Chinese were coming of age. The Mission was filled to the brim with refugees from El Salvador, Nicaragua and Honduras, people who were escaping the CIA, John Negroponte, Oliver North, and Elliot Abrams' plots to destroy them in their own countries. They moved to the United States, hoping to fight the repression back in their own Third World countries, under the red, white and blue American flag, and under the nose of the demented Uncle Sam.

Alongside all of this political activity was the emerging gay political and economic clout. This was brought to center stage by Milk when he called for boycotts of Florida Orange Juice and the Coors Brewing Company. By working with Cesar Chavez, he solidified the labor vote. Oddly, the old guard homosexual power base did not elect Harvey Milk. Harvey was way too far to the left for the Gayourgeoisie. They didn't like him until he was dead.

Labor elected Harvey Milk Supervisor, alongside votes from Preservationists, Blacks, Street Gays, Dykes on Bikes, community activists, and 60s Rice and Beans Leftovers from the Haight who were still recovering from bad drugs and CIA plots to take over the world. Once again, politics had changed San Francisco.

The Gayourgeoisie and their real estate speculators came into the community of grand illusions from their ivory towers to buy, buy, and buy and then just as rapidly sell, sell, and sell. It ruined the world we had. Prices went through the ceiling. They started calling themselves "Gay Professionals"—whatever that means. Yet for the artists, the ones who had been there first, rents quickly became unaffordable. Activists were sickened by the conspicuous marketing of greed and power. As the neighborhood's color faded and everything went commercial, the Gayourgeoisie sold the rainbow to the highest bidder who was probably wearing a buff All American Boy tee-shirt. The artists who had made the neighborhood what it was were forced to slowly move on. All American Boy was the first "Clone" menswear shop on Castro Street.

Of course there's always money to be made on sex. In this case, new trends in gender and sexual identification and that contradiction helped cover up some subtleties of the changes going on in plain sight. Even so, dirty little stories of betrayal and exploitation of blood in the streets for ill-gotten gain were on everyone's lips. Even now my friends have asked me when I began writing these stories: "Princess, you're not going to tell them what I did? Are you Princess?" Talking about sex, or sex and money, or men in dresses, or political intrigue, drugs and power are, as we all know, such a messy business.

Speaking of "messy business," probably the biggest misconception in the American mass consciousness concerning homosexual men and women is that deep down we really desire to be the opposite gender. This is absolutely not true unless it is. I, for example have never wanted to have a baby or a period, nor have I met a lesbian who wanted balls to scratch. It would be more appropriate to say that I am comfortable with the vulnerable varieties of the energy I have within me. There are some who are not and they may wish to change everything about their gender—and sometimes they actually do, with remarkable and glorious success. It was just theatre for me.

The eclectic dressing of the early seventies was all about bringing together the male and female, the yin and yang energies within ourselves, not as opposite energies but as manifestations of oneness. This is a journey not of going toward the often referenced unifying white light of the eastern traditions, but to splintering into light that breaks wide and glitters in a multitude of colors. Personally, I prefer red light, especially once I reached a 32-inch waist and beyond. And when I die, I plan to go toward the Red Light—White Light is a trick! The famous glittered beards, evening gowns and black leather of the period were just an outward manifestation of that balancing act of gender and light. In reality, there is no more masculine act than two men making love to each other.

We were in the heyday of the sexual revolution. We were sexual warriors. We had more sex than anyone, anywhere, ever–and the bewildered mainstream said they wanted to make it all go away when, in reality, they were screaming jealous.

This decade-long party was 2,000 years in the making and no one but royalty attended and, naturally for me, Cock was King! I took the plunge into the sexuality of the seventies with the same fervor as an ambitious individual seeking a prosperous career. Countless roles were there to be played. There were slaves, masters and lovers, both young and old. All were welcome as part of the experimentation, exploration and endless need for satisfaction that had been denied for centuries, previously suppressed under the guise of false morality and religion.

Religion and politics, sex and politics, sex and religion were all in bed together. The creatures of the night that prowled in the shadows—in the belly of Market Street, and the parks, beaches, abandoned buildings, busy department stores, alleys, sewers, bathhouses and glory holes South of Market—were the same creatures who in daylight worked in the citadels of power, in institutions that claimed moral righteousness with snarky attitudes where they toiled in well-appointed suites during the day but caroused wantonly by night swinging from slings at the Barracks bathhouse as their drugs kicked in.

From casual blow jobs in the corporate offices atop the Bank of America Building, to torrid encounters in the corridors of the State and Federal Buildings, from the Market Street tunnels of the yet-to-be finished Bay Area Rapid Transit, to the City Hall Dome or under the cross of the cathedrals themselves—there was politics, sex, corruption, sex and more sex, both good and bad. We made the Oval Office ready for sex.

In this book, I have jotted down glimpses into this remarkable period when we radically broke with past conventions. It's true that we were creating a new reality and yet the lives of the artists who passed through The Hula Palace Salons mirrored those of all the great artists of times past.

We were heavenly players living a dream: life as art. We were Children of Paradise. We lived our lives like classic characters playing out scenes, whether they ranged from the dark depths of Caligula or Genet to those from Dr. Seuss and Disney.

To paraphrase and gender bend a quote from the Madwoman of Chaillot: "A Lady must change her name as often as her hat: on the hour." We did just that. We all had many exotic and common names and wore so many hats. Identity was remarkably fluid. You met someone as one person in the afternoon for a casual blow job, then saw him again that night at dinner with his wife, knowing he had totally separate lives—and neither of you missed a beat.

Looking out the Hula Palace Salon's third floor bay window, at the corner of 590 Castro and 19th Streets, I had my own private view of a very public sexual revolution. I would sit, fan, and watch beautiful boys saunter by while sitting in my Queen's Wicker from early morn and through the day and night. They walked, I fanned. I watched them turn into men. And sometimes we fucked. Some even became my Prince for a while, and once—after an interlude with a Duke— Princess Etta felt that at least for that evening, I was a Duchess.

14

* * * * *

San Francisco was new, fresh, an exciting Petri dish of luscious filth. There were new Gay bars reflecting various sexual tastes and desires such as Toad Hall, The Pendulum, and the popular Midnight Sun. New places arose ranging from a fabulous gay bookstore named Paperback Traffic along with a dark nasty hole called the Jaguar Adult Books, complete with a playroom in the back for quick encounters and instant weekend marriages.

Painters painting, poets in the streets, music in the air, and dancing were everywhere. Did we ever dance! Isadora Duncan would have been proud. After all, she had lived in The Castro and The Mission as a child, at a time when Gertrude Stein was growing up, just across the Bay in Oakland.

Theater was alive and well and everywhere. It could be found on the streets, in the salons, small houses, basements, garages and old firehouses. There must have been hundreds of venues. New material was being written constantly. New lines, new colors and new attitudes with new twists on reality poured on to the streets. We were having an informal costume ball and everyone was invited.

Little did we know that by 1978 all of this would change just as abruptly?

Anita Bryant, Pat Buchanan, Gay Bashing, Mass Murders in Guyana, The Briggs Initiative, the Assassinations of Mayor George Moscone and Supervisor Harvey Milk by Dan White, Dianne Feinstein's Lap Dog, The Trial, The White Night Riot, Robert Opel's murder, the attempts on my life, the AIDS pandemic, suicides, and more funerals than we could even count. San Francisco would reel from joy to sorrow, from victory to defeat, from bright colored flowers in the window boxes to Gay Widows in mourning on floats in parades throughout the streets. We were now on the other side of forever.

All of this happened while the "Politically Correct" maggots were everywhere, trying to profit from the sorrow of a lost dream, a dream that left many of us dead and/or damaged goods, now searching for a new place to call home. Sometimes, I refer to that despicable Gayourgeoisie as "Lizards" even though in real life I actually love reptiles.

Warren Hinkel of the San Francisco Examiner and the author of Gay Slayer asked why no one within the gay community has ever spoken out on all the conspiracy theories on the assassinations, murders, and HIV/AIDS.

I am here to say we did speak out.

And when we did we were either threatened into silence or murdered like

Robert Opel. Yes, the Lizards could get away with anything in San Francisco, including murder.

But now the time has come to lift the veil on the Gay Seventies.

We all know how Harvey Milk was murdered but do you know why?

As you read, once again, please remember that the volume of characters is so vast that some consolidation of the main personages was required.

Even time itself is warped to conform to the conventional idea of day and night.

Everything happened and nothing had happened at all.

And just because everything was real, it didn't mean things were as they appeared. Believe nothing because it is all too true.

I remember how the sun came up early every morning in an endless repetition for dancers at the end of time. Why would anyone try so hard to stop it?

What happened? You'll have to read on …

THE ADVOCATE

A DIVISION OF LIBERATION PUBLICATIONS, INC.

15 June 1992

Dear Lee,

Thank you for sharing these wonderful stories with me. Do continue on with the project; ten or 12 stories could very well make a book, not to mention a necessary adjustment of gay history.

I appreciate you staying in touch.
All best until we next speak.

Mark Thompson

Lee Mentley, Les Plush front parlor Hula Palace. Photo by Para

MY ARRIVAL

Can I Even
Begin
To Reach Inside
Touch My Soul
Yes!
Here These People!
This City

*I*t's 1972 and we, the boy and girls at The Hula Palace, have just finished painting our Hula Palace Victorian kitchen adjoining the dining salon. I'm happy to report I didn't even break a nail!

I love this sweet yellow. It looks great against the 1950s red felt Mexican jacket sported by a cute little Burro wearing a sequined sombrero. I found the little gem at Purple Heart Thrift Store for a quarter. La kitchen motif was chosen from two colors in Fiestaware scrounged and purchased at Saint Vincent de Paul on Folsom Street. Not the brightly colored Mexican late 40s palette all queens love to kill for. No, it was a more softly refined 50s pastel, like Melmac. We screamed over the creamy yellow, cooing over the robin's egg blue. It was a striking complement to the curtain-patterned house dresses and pursed red lips we boys loved to don around the salon, even sharing them with the world at Cala, our local supermarket.

Linda sniffed out "authentic" 1950s Spanish decals at Cliff's Variety Store, right from old man Ernie, our handsome hero of hardware. He had saved all his merchandise since the turn of the century in its original packaging, bless his heart. If you decide to decorate by any period, you could find whatever you needed from Ernie who always wore black and we dubbed him "Zorro." Ms. Lawn placed wet, kitsch decals on the white tiles above the kitchen sink. What a glorious June day! Earth girls are so easy to please. Indeed, how Gay we truly were!

Etta, HRH Princess—that would be me—arranged a High Contempo Tea Party to show off our manly handy work and our new dresses. I never figured out what Etta Linda meant by "High Contempo Tea" but then she was raised in Sacramento's

Pristine Condition. Photo by Walker L. Dukes

suburbs. We invited our dearest lady of the night, Mona Mandrake (but she never comes out during the day). And, of course, the showgirls from Cockettes including the adorable dizzy Gemini Pristine Condition, Philthee Ritz, and Kreemah Ritz; one of the "Boom Boom Girls" Dolores Deluxe; our Baltimore friends Divine and Mink Stole; and the ever-gorgeous David Baker Junior, who was popularly known as Thumper and we know why! In other words, David was a gorgeous man with a big dick! I'll never forget the exquisite nude ballet David performed in the counterculture satirical horror musical Vice Palace staring his lover Divine at the infamous Palace Theatre in North Beach. This offbeat, off-off-off Broadway, off-the-edge, blood-soaked musical was based on Edgar Allen Poe's Masque of the Red Death gone Blame It on the Bossa Nova.

But I digress. Tonight, we put together this casual event to showcase our new salon décor, serving Chinese tea, fondue, pot, and some sexy crackers everything was sexy back then! This feast was about all we could afford, but it did not lack for glamour!

And we cannot forget The Drag itself. As my alter-ego ELA, a spicy jalapeño drag queen from East L.A. I'm forever thankful that all those sweet little full-bodied old ladies from Pasadena and their counterparts the stately matrons from San Francisco who went on to their reward leaving us their finest garments via Sally Ann's in Los Angeles, or Purple Heart and Saint Vincent's in San Francisco or any other secondhand stores we would find hitchhiking between our two cosmic un-identical homes. As Uncle Nicky would say, "There was a time when men were men, and so were half the women." &…, I got me all their delicate fashions and dainties for a thin dime

Flaunting a full display of color, I wore a pastel green, small flowered print silk rayon summer dress found on a fast dash with Ms. Forest Lawn—we were always on a cosmic shopping spree of one sort or another. I think we were meditating at Rose Hill Mausoleum when we channeled a new thrift shop on Colorado Boulevard. Many of my "Sophia Loren'esque" evening gowns came from a shop owned by a lovely woman who had collected the closets of all those who had conveniently died in Pasadena so I could look good. Yet it was Pérez who stole the show, wearing a 30s black satin gown with a sequined peacock draped down the front. This dress really belonged to me. Sadly, it would meet a woeful end. In the future, she would confess that—like most of my best drag—the gown had been ripped off her back in a drunken sexual frenzy à la Bimbo's New Year's Eve extravaganza hosted by John Rothermel and Sylvester in North Beach. The Bitch was stealing my act! No wonder, she was a woman to behold and radiant in my drag! It made me SAD.

Anyway, I was running around with an underground musical gang at that time called The Mourners. We did publicity stunts with an underground theatrical troupe, The Tap Dancing Fools, for RCA and the dark romance of Laura Nyro. We loved the dead, meaning we played funerals, hung out in cemeteries, and did photo sessions with headstones. In Ronald Reagan's 60s California, cemeteries were the only places to be safe at night. We hung out at The Troubadour on Santa Monica, to stunt for Ms. Nyro and drink with Jack Nicholson at the bar. Ms. Lawn was always lifting her skirts and flashing Jack.

In any case, back to the salon.

Etta borrowed my soft pink crepe with small white polka dots. She wore her lavish blonde hair down with cute iridescent pink barrettes at the side. She's so neo-conservative, very Susie Q. What a delightful memory tonight will make. Etta was excited. It was the first time she would entertain Divine. Divine had stopped by only once, with Goldie, when I gave her my tiara and we went off shopping at City of Paris, then had our-nails-done at Magnin's mezzanine.

Etta didn't remember Divine's visit saying I was a dirty little liar and a star fucker. In any case, I had recently received very bad news but now I only wanted to be happy. So we were happy—not boring and maudlin. Truly Gay in fact!

I asked Etta if Iory, our Tibetan princess, was coming. She said, "No, he is off writing tales of Science Fiction Drag Queens based on Hula Palace hoopla. She is calling the book Naughty Astronautess." "Well," I quipped, 'She should know something about that, having blasted off the planet long ago."

The bell rang. Someone was at the scrolling metal gate, ubiquitous in San Francisco of this era, waiting to enter the Hula Palace. We went to the landing to greet our guests. We could see them dragging themselves up the two flights in overworked heels.

"Aloha, Girls."

"Hi Princess, Hi Etta!"

"Aloha, Divine."

"Oh, I love the dresses."

"Mahalo plenty."

"Hi, Girls. Aloha."

"OOOH Mink, you look so good."

"Welcome to the Hula Palace."

Ton's of Clatter Chatter ...,

"Kissie Kissie."

"Good to see you, dallings."

"I heard that gruff giggle, it must be La Ritz."

"Where did you get that dress?"

"In High School in Pasadena."

"Girl ...!" And on and on it went! Clatter, Chatter ...

Divine wore her traditional white flight suit and those black silver vintage 50s springalators. Mink's mercurochrome-red hair flowed by, 50s cat's eye specs turned up. Kreemah followed in tow, styled as High Matron with a splendid hat that she said she had it made downtown. "Or, maybe it was stolen from the Fillmore Salvation Army," I teased as he growled at me. "I know you would never do a thing like that."

"I'm not one of those kinds of girls," she responded. Together, we both cried out "Those Bad Girls!" Yet honestly, she was exactly that sort of girl!

Pristine Condition was late as usual. It would be hard for me, too, to get out of bed on time if I were living with Billy Orchid smoking Angel Dust all the time. I'd never get out the door. Pristine would show up finally with the adorably buxom Dolores DeLux. We were all so lovely. Thumper wore his basket bulging, skin-tight black leathers and big polished boots. You know how a handsome man at high tea causes a stir. I had wished that Billy were coming but he had been commissioned for a painting and Prissy said she couldn't drag him away from the studio, not even for high tea with Princess ELA Lee. There would be an unveiling of his newest work in about a week, in his studio coinciding with his wedding to Cupie Doll the human art work of pure dementia he met in a stoned hallucination. The Girls from The Hula Palace invited themselves. Yay!

As I write this, another memory comes to mind: how delightfully clever we had all been at the Bakery Café opening.

The Hula Palace had organized a celebration of entertainment for the lovely Don and Steve, owners of Paperback Traffic Bookstore. They had purchased two rundown Victorians near the Sausage Factory and renovated them, transforming them into The Eureka Arcade. It was a wonderful collection of curiosity shops selling body oils, fragrant soaps, European and African imports, books and art, and included The Bakery Café, a restaurant with an outdoor covered deck and lovely garden designed by another tall hunk artist, Jack Buehler. This was a real treasure for the community. Donny and Stevie had done a good job. Sadly, this was the beginning of the horrific gentrification of The Castro.

I gave Divine my sassy mahalo, a Hawaiian "Thank you very much," for making a guest appearance plus autographing all those Heart Break of Psoriasis posters. Heart Break was Divine's mainstream stage début. She played a disgruntled average mom turned gun moll in a musical setting. It bombed miserably at the Kabuki Theatre. I could never figure out why, since after all, it was delightfully strange. I especially thanked her for autographing one of the props, a seashell box," To The Girls at the Hula Palace, Love Divine." I will always treasure it.

The seashell box came from a Philthee Ritz rewrite of a Broadway play Ladies in Retirement, a 30s British murder mystery. The Upper Market Street Gallery had produced the revival under the name The Metronome Murders. Divine was brilliant as the evil auntie. She starred with her six-foot-six Frederick's of Hollywood Cockette drag queen sidekick, Goldie Glitters, playing Divine's spinster sister, along with the lovely Jano Roland as the quintessential maid and the unforgettable superstar Mink Stole as the unfortunate victim. It was directed by Dr. Queen, Martin Worman of the Cockettes, who was known as Philthee Ritz.

Divine and Goldie played two elderly sisters that kill their benefactor for the man, the house, the money, or something like that. In the course of the play Divine collected seashells on the English seashore which she slowly glued to the top of a cedar box while she and Goldie plotted their evil way through the melodrama. An aside: Goldie eventually became the first male homecoming queen at Santa Monica City College. Yes, she did!

Anyway, I received the little gem of a box for Christmas, from my ever-chic roommate Ravenous Rachel. Rachel was buttering me up because she wanted my white nouveau sculpted head of an African Goddess, although she'll never get it!

Metronome was the most astounding experience in theater I'd had seen since witnessing Divine as reigning queen in the Miss Demeanor Pageant. Her monologue at the pageant was so hysterical I eventually fell on the floor, wet my skirt, and begged to be strangled to death. It started with how Divine stole her first bottle of hair dye at age six, which leads her into a life of crime, making her the first meglo-homocidal artist, culminating in the Tate Murders. The theme of the entire evening was "crimes of passion." The entire star-studded cast was smashing.

The whole evening was a fundraiser for two zany Cockettes who had crashed blindly into a antique lamppost in front of the Fairmont Hotel, or was it the St. Francis. Does it really matter? Handsome Daniel and the exotic Gary Cherry had to come up with $25,000 dollars to pay for the damages or go to jail.

The Cockettes booked the infamous House of Good, which eventually became The Jim Jones People's Temple, and put on a "Miss Demeanor Pageant" just to help their sisters out in their time of need. They were all such good kids. Etta was in that one too. She got third place as "Miss Peace Love." Her crime was singing a medley from Hair. China White or maybe it was violinist Naomi Ruth Eisenberg, who once sang with her lover Dan Hicks and his band The Hot Licks, won first prize. In any case, whoever it was, she was then arrested on the Golden Gate Bridge on her way home from the pageant. The police accused her of being intoxicated and confiscated her hypodermic syringe ear rings. Life? Art? It's all blurring together.

Metronome Murder was the first time I experienced Glenn playing any other character than Divine. What an artist! We all loved Divine. She was our deity of wrathful compassion…but in good shoes!

Back to the present: I showed Divine the cedar, seashell treasure prominently displayed on the salon mantel. "Yes, Princess, it's terrific. I didn't know what had happened to it after the play. I loved doing that mystery."

I then asked the tough question: "You didn't enjoy Heart Break though did you?"

"Well at first I did. And then no, all I wanted to do was leave town."

"Sorry, doll. You should have done that extra time-step Mona Mandrake taught you for the shopping mall number. Like Pola said, you would have brought the house down and it would have saved you the whole undeserved miserable experience." We chuckled.

"Someday I will do a fabulous musical on the big screen," Divine responded.

"You will my dear, you will!" I concurred.

Mink patted Glenn's hand. "Mink, did you enjoy the Bakery Cafe opening?"

"Yes, what a wonderful day it was. And what a pleasant surprise it was for Lily Tomlin to join us at the Arcade. "

"She's so tiny."

"Isn't she though."

I first met Lily Tomlin the night before the opening of the Arcade at a Democratic Women's fund raiser. We played Blackjack. San Francisco Supervisor Dianne Feinstein had dealt us both bad hands. Fein-

Lily Tomlin; Sister Ed; Divine and Pristine Condition at an autograph party for Divine at the grand opening of the Bakery Cafe hosted by the Hula Palace on Castro; 1975. Photo by Daniel Nicoletta

stein was drinking vodka gimlets and smoking something minty green, all I could remember was dandruff on her cheap black chemise and the look on Lily's face.

I decided to take a chance and invited Lily to the Eureka Arcade opening. I mentioned that Angel of Light, Sister Ed, who was the only American to ever perform with the Peking Opera, she spoke perfect Chinese, was going to do an impersonation of Lily's famous character Ernestine. I told her that Divine would be there to sign autographs, and that Pristine Condition and Etta would be singing those songs that you're always ashamed to ask for like "The Lion Sleeps Tonight." Beyond that, Sandy Counts who played Pan at the Renaissance Fairs would be performing on his tightrope above the lovely garden. Lily said she would try and make it. I thought to myself, "Sure, she will. She's probably seen a thousand queens do Ernestine." Then she told me that friends of hers were opening a gallery called 'Uptown' in the Arcade and that she would love to see them succeed. So maybe she would indeed come.

I was absolutely delighted when she did show. She has been on the road with her one woman show and so she said it was time for her to see what people did during the day. She was so pale, but we just love Lilly. It was wonderful.

Back to the Hula Palace present ...

"What the hell were you doing at a democratic fundraiser?" Kreemah quipped as she went off to the kitchen to assist Etta with the tea.

Etta chimed in. "You know how political ELA is during the day. Remember he did head up the Young Americans for Robert Kennedy."

"Really Girlfriend", are you really bringing this up?

I don't like to talk about it but I was at the Ambassador Hotel the night RFK was shot. And let's not forget that six other people went to the hospital that night. By the way, how did that happen with one gunman? When the pictures came out in Life magazine from that night, I saw myself with Sirhan Sirhan standing right behind me. So, NO! ... I don't like to talk about it.

"Tell us more, Lee Lee."

"Kreemah, you be good in there. Stop asking me to talk about death or we'll throw another farewell party." I leaned into Divine; redheads gossiping in the kitchen can be lethal.

"Spell the name right, Girls!" Warned Divine to Goldie.

Mink turned to me and asked, "What farewell party?"

"Ohhhhhh, well ... Kreemah tried a move to Ft. Lauderdale to escape her reputation so we had a little event for her here at the Hula Palace. She lasted six months in south Florida then returned." I looked to Divine and whispered, "Her act didn't play there."

Divine murmured "Hmmmmm."

"I heard that, you queens!" Kreemah shouted back.

"You were supposed too!"

Unfortunately for Kreemah, that party was held the same day as Cockette Link's wake after his sudden, tragic, and untimely death in Southeast Asia. Link had supposedly been hit by a car and mysteriously died in the hospital, although everyone thought it might actually have been connected to a corrupt government official and involved opium smuggling. I am sure the angels just swooped him up at the right time.

Anyway, we were asked by Cockettes Lizzy and Wally if they could have a private wake at The Hula Palace. They wanted to give away Link's possessions, everything left in his recently returned steamer trunk to his colorful theatrical sisters. We placed the trunk in Etta's receiving salon for the mourners and put Kreemah in the front parlor to liven everyone up after the ritual for dear Link.

Etta had been eavesdropping and yelled from the kitchen, "Remember how smashed I got on champagne at the wake and upset poor beautiful Lizzy?"

"Oh that's right; she was so upset and screamed at you. But what could she expect? After all, it was a going away party for both of them."

"I don't know. I honestly never understood why she was upset."

Divine sweetly stood on ceremony, saying how sad it was to go so young. Then she asked me about my mother. I asked, "Can we dish? Mothers!"

Divine and Goldie Glitters had met my mother Sarah on Castro Street. Mom recognized them from Todd Trexler's posters. She introduced herself and invited them to breakfast at Castro Cafe. They became immediate friends. Soon thereafter, without warning, mom moved to Las Vegas with a new Latin lover.

"Have you met him...?" Gawd, had I.

One night I flew into LA. from Hawai'i, just in time to see Bette Midler deliver a great concert at Universal. I was coming to LA to deliver a jewelry commission I created while in the islands. My client was so pleased he gave me two tickets and a limo for my stay in LA LA Land. I went over to my drag sister Ms. Maroon's to borrow some Hollywood frocks. I found out she was going to the Midler concert, too, along with her love bug Uncle Louis who would end up managing the Pointer Sisters. We were all going—Two Limos and Three Pointer Sisters!

I went into East L.A. to share aloha with mom and to see if she wanted to join us. I was in my white Jamaican slacks with a little black and white polkadot scarf, halter top, black pearls, and my long black sable. I wanted to show off my perfectly tanned body. I was getting out of the limo in the parking lot of our family's sleazy liquor store. Mom had just arrived with her new beau. She introduced me to "Mr. Kmart" right there on the spot. I nearly died but I tried to hide my dismay under my Oleg Cassini. I couldn't help it; my claws were showing. I blurted out, "But Mommy, look at him, he shops at K-Mart! Mom!" I was distraught. My mom has somehow run off with Mr. K-Mart. What was I going to do? I'd rather see her with trailer trash than someone who thinks he is upscale off Whittier Boulevard at K-Mart.

"That's Okay, Princess," the Hula Palace Queens responded to my tale. "Your mom knows what she is doing. She's no dumb bunny. Is he handsome at least?"

"Maybe. If you can get past the labels and Butch Wax."

"So no problem, Princess. She's having a ball, especially since she loves Vegas."

Etta entered with light pupus. "Princess, are you talking about your off-beat family again? Isn't it time you just did a hula and entertained the girls?"

"What off-beat family member are you talking about now?" Kreemah asked.

"Mommy." The doorbell rang.

"Tell them about your hillbilly, gun–toting Auntie Maria"

"Etta, Dalling, get the door."

Etta loved to talk about my poor dear Aunty Marie who once gave her a fright when she saw her carrying a 45. I grew up in a Spanish ghetto so what can I tell you: the whole family had guns. We lived in the Wild West. Personally I find Aunty an inspiration. Etta thinks she's a little shaky but really she's just very creative. After all, she spends a lot of time all alone out in the country near Ojai.

Aunty lived down the hill from Johnny Cash in Casita Springs. Uncle Curly was a country-western singer who played on the road for weeks at a time. She didn't like to be alone; so she created mannequins by stuffing old clothes as company. She positioned them, sitting up, at her outdoor picnic table, or scattered them around her yard. She played cards with them and had her coffee or drank a beer with them. It made her feel good. That way she was not alone.

They could be seen from the roadway. That way friends and even strangers going by thought that she had company. This, she told me, keeps the Koko Man away. I believe her.

"The Koko Man, Princess ?"

"The Mexican Boogie Man, Etta !"

"Oh, Princess!"

Anyway, for me, her behavior isn't that of a sicko—it's being creative. Where do you think I learned to decorate and win at cards? Still, she does carry a gun which freaks Etta out.

"Stop shaking your finger at me and open the door, before the guests go away!"

"We should be so lucky."

The doorbell rang again. It was Pristine Condition and the sexy Deluxe. Pristine was spinning in her shoes as usual and yelling, "Princess, you better have that necklace ready. Where's my new drag?" Prissy had convinced me to create some fun wearable baby toys for her next Valentine's show.

"I have them, dalling."

She hugged and kissed around and screamed while spinning with her hands in the air. "We are the ladies who brunch!"

Etta offered Deluxe, who was pulling up the rear, something cold to drink. She was so exhausted from keeping up with Pristine she immediately sank into the wicker to recoup her strength.

Where's Mink?

She's with Thumper in the front salon looking at the new erotic sketches from the Marquee, Jim Campbell. "Come, let's go see," said Etta as she pulled her back up from the comfy chair and scooted off with the Deluxe down the hall.

Prissy was modeling her new jewels from The Princess's workshop. Prissy worked every vanity mirror in the Palace, all the while singing "Where the boys are, I will be there too." Meanwhile, Divine, Goldie et al. chatted the afternoon away dishing on the lessons of being Big Bad Gurls. After a bit more gaiety and refreshment, they all slowly departed for the very late afternoon.

I changed into something butch and grabbed my handbag. I needed some distraction. You see, just before tea, I had found out that a boyhood sweetheart had died. We had been lovers for over ten years. My Mom had written me and it seems he had been stabbed at a party in East L.A. I didn't want to bring it up at brunch and spoil everyone's fun. There was really no one to console me. No one at home in ELA ever knew we were lovers. Only Etta knew what had happened. "Go for a walk," he suggested as she went for a nap himself. "She's so frail from too many salads," I thought, "but pink really does suit her."

I went down and sat at the foot of the steps to watch the boys cruise by, then walked down to the Midnight Sun, our neighborhood bar, to look for some fun. I needed some bun watching to clear my head. The interior of the Midnight Sun was designed as a circus. Wonderful carnival images had been painted by the Upper Market Street gang. Paul the Clown was there and we chatted about Shakespeare's Twelfth Night. We had played star-crossed lovers, my Sir Toby to his exotic Maria. We laughed at how his particular clown was an After Dark model by day and an old Elizabethan hag stable woman by night, and how I was a Princess with a beard. We wondered if that made us lesbian lovers?

After a few shooters with Paul and our very own Oberon—Cowboy Cirby—tending bar, I eventually sat on the beer cases in the corner, alone and depressed, leaning against a fucking wall. I wrote poetic lines in my sketchpad. I tried to focus on the fun I had this afternoon. I wrote one for Divine:

Elephants in sky pulling coach Divine,

Flaming across heavens,

Screaming mockeries over land,

Flattening islands, leaving sand.

Then I wrote one for my lost love, for my sweet, departed friend. I'll always remember how he would sneak out at night, climb up on the roof into my window, then slip into my bed to make sweaty pubescent love to me. Sometimes we made passionate love in the back of his father's 47 Plymouth. I had tried to convince him to move to San Francisco, to get out of the ghetto, but he couldn't picture himself outside of East LA culture. Now that his sweet spirit had taken flight, I wrote a poem; The Kite:

There are men that are kites that are made of men.

There is a man on the kite, the kite is a man.

This made me even bluer. I had really received a double whammy in the mail today. My recently confused boyfriend from L.A., Shad, had sent me a "Dear Princess" letter that read in part: "Although we were instantly devoted, we were also condemned to a life together, or apart, void of ignorance, and fraught with truth, bitterness and subliminal hate." What was he talking about? "We were to be mental lovers," he wrote. What could this mean? "We had all sacrificed innocence for self-awareness." What was this crap? This boy needed help—Mormons?

I casually walked up Castro Street to Tommy's Plants. It was just getting dark and the cool breeze was coming over Twin Peaks. I loved the fog and the smell of the sea. It made everything feel so fresh and alive.

I knocked on Tommy's door but he wasn't in. He was probably at Toad Hall. I wanted to apologize to him for what our dear always-in-trouble roommate Jimbo did last week.

Etta had found Tommy standing on the top steps of the Hula Palace. He had followed a trail of dirt that had dropped from a plant Jimbo had stolen from the front of The Plant Shop. Etta and Tommy found Jimbo sprawled out in a Quaalude dream with his arms wrapped around the poor suffering ficus. I decided I'd stop by Tommy's tomorrow, and not walk back down to Toad Hall although Tommy was always nasty fun to see.

I went on to 590. I climbed the two flights of stairs to the Hula Palace and opened the door. "I'm home!" I cried out.

It was silent—too silent—as I listened to the awkward silence, poised for any disturbing noises. I could smell trouble in the air. I slowly walked up the stairs and into the dining salon where I found Etta quietly steaming in the dark.

Upset and sulking in the queen's green wicker, still in her little pink dress, adorned by her tight virginal curls. Yet she was breathing fire. She told me that Rachel—the bitch that lived in the front all–white salon, with her white satin sheets, white wicker, white phone, and with his Crystal Queen attitude, the kind that cared most about a lifestyle of suburban comforts than anything else—had confined her suffering white Afghan Rona to her white bed. This was utterly inhumane white dog decor that had arrived from Gumps the chi chi department store downtown.

"She never gets anywhere, she only arrives," Etta screamed through her teeth. "Shortly after high tea, Rachel got back from wherever. She changed into her new white caftan. Then, with her twin Taurian bitch sister roommate, Ms. Blue, they both paraded into the kitchen. They were dismayed at the tea pot and cups in the sink. They were terribly rude and called me a dirty little bitch. So I yelled, 'Fuck you queens!' and they stormed off to their white ward, with me screaming after them. I'm so sick of this fashionable anglophile shit."

Trouble in paradise! Yet I knew this spat was coming. There was no aloha between these queens. Rachel was so insistent on being perfect and neat and promoting what she saw as stylish. Basically I saw her as a hopeless missionary, an ambassador for stupid white people, whereas Etta & I, the Princess, we were the unfortunate Polynesians she was dying to convert.

I hated to see Etta like this. No matter what I did I couldn't stop her from steaming. She had taken this all so seriously and I would soon learn why. I went into my room to put on my summer dress. I reappeared as The Princess. I was looking good!

I wanted to forget all about my blue depression I'd felt at the Midnight Sun. I offered Etta some Valium, but Etta was feeling too perfect for drugs. Thinking that it would cheer her up I did a quick little "Sophisticated Hula." This got her up out of the chair and into a better mood. We started to tidy up the kitchen. I started by washing the tea party dishes.

It was classic battle between "I Ching Etta" with her Zen brown rice on one hand and our Suburban Faux European idiot with caviar tastes on the other. Just FYI, personally I love caviar with just about anything, especially peanut butter, celery, or strawberries; you don't have to shop Uptown to enjoy fine cuisine, you know.

Etta swept the floor, all the while endlessly dishing Rachel or Blue. She's this, he's that and so forth.

Then—like peaking on a tab of acid—I finally really heard her. I realized that Etta was right. Rachel wanted to turn the whole fucking world into white décor. Not just the walls, the sheets, the phone, the mantle, the rugs, or the dog. I said, "Etta, she wants it all—our rooms, our drag and our lives to be all white too."

"You're right, Princess" We freaked. We would be next: white from head to toe. Oh God! What could we do?

We looked at each other. "She has to go! Ms. Blue too. This is WAR!"

That's when Etta dropped the first dish. I smiled. We looked at the broken fiesta blue on the floor. Etta smiled. We knew what we had to do. Rachel loved this stuff. She marveled at how pretty it was when I found it. But the Princess had also paid for it—so we could destroy it if we wanted to. "Just throw it into the trash."

"No, let's break everything!"

"Okay, Queen." I went for the dish drain. Etta went for the pantry for the pots and pans and the floor was soon a pile of rubble. I love excitement and drama. "Break it, break it, and break it all!" This would get her. Vintage collectables on to the floor, cups out the window, pots and pans into the trash and silver ware in the air!

Then we got our best idea: we dragged the kitchen table in front of the stove and then turned on all the burners and blowing out the flames.

With the oven door open, I took the brightly colored 40s cafe tablecloth and wrapped it on my head like a babushka. Etta opened the front of her dress to expose his hairy chest. We climbed up on top of the table and began, like two women with stigmata, to wail and weep. This reminded me of being at home with my Italian Gypsy Aunts.

"Mama Mia!" "Guadalupe!" "We have been so bad!" "Forgive us!" We cried openly. We confessed our sins of sloth and filth. We lamented how we were so beyond help that there was no alternative but to kill ourselves for having dirtied the sink. We became hysterical with crocodile tears. All we needed was some catsup and we could have passed for having a spontaneous divine revelation. "Where's my rosary when I need it?" "Guadalupe, help us" Were we laughing? Were we crying? The Uncle Ben and Aunt Jemima salt and pepper shakers were shaken tonight. Wow, this was fun!

Etta wasn't depressed anymore.

"Mama Mia!" "Guadalupe!" and "Forgive Us!"

Rachel, of course, could not have ignored the commotion in the kitchen. She appeared at the kitchen door for a short, timid moment. We pretended we didn't notice his spying. She peered in at us and freaked out as he saw the broken mess on the floor. What she had seen really disturbed her. Her white little mind was ticking. This wasn't a problem shopping could solve. What would he do? Poor Rachel, seeing this vision of lonely, pathetic hairy women, demonstrating their willingness to sacrifice anything to deflate their own ugly sister's stupid fucking white perfectionist habits. Naturally, she quickly removed herself (as we knew she would) back to her white ward in his best Loretta Young full-skirt twirl. This was our sign from God!

Etta and I powdered up and went out for dinner down at the Sausage Factory, where we celebrated with some good dark burgundy.

"The game is afoot, Etta"

"What else should we do?"

"We could overfeed Rona, that poor pathetic dog, and ruin her waist line."

"Rachel would shit if she owned a fat doggie."

"That poor dog is just like Greta Garbo: always afraid to go out. Rachel has to drag her out the door just to do her business."

"We could shave Rona like a poodle and say we didn't know how it happened."

"Leave the dog alone ELA," Etta worries too much.

"We could get Rachel 'luded out and tattoo her nasty white ass? Or we could put Deep Heat into her lube?" Oooooh, now that's interesting, Etta!"

Ultimately, what we could really count on when the chips came down was having our handsome cowboy roommate Robert's vote. We had already won and Rachel didn't know it. Rachel would hang herself with her own mouth. Robert wasn't going tell his butch numbers that he lived at a Blue Swan Hotel. This was going to be sweet.

"Girl Fight!"

"More wine, Dearie?"

"We will write a play, ELA, we will call it War of Decor or As the Lava Flows."

"Tomorrow we'll shop for new dinnerware. I'm registered at the Saint Vincent de Paul Thrift Shop you know."

Next morning Rachel announced there was to be a House Meeting.

I instantly went to my closet and returned as "Our Miss Brooks," wearing a regulation Den Mother's uniform, complete with swagger stick in hand. Etta fanned while I laid the cards on the table. I didn't want to waste any time. I went straight for the throat. I said, "Robert, ask Rachel what she thinks about your biker numbers. How about that hot dude you met at the clinic? Tom Smith, I think, was his name. Go on Rachel, tell Robert what you think of his tricks, and his messy room and nasty looking men." This was followed by much

Hula Palace Salon Tui. Flyer by Jim Campbell

screaming and trying to convince dear Robert that he should live more like us, our version of "That Gurls" if you will. Robert quickly got the Big Picture of where this was heading.

After a scolding from the handsome cowboy about getting real, Rachel backed down. She knew it was over. Robert loved Rachel— but Robert loved his dirty, nasty, heavy-duty men more! As did we all. As long as Robert was residing here, we knew that his men would be flowing in a steady stream, allowing us to cruise our own hallway. We were, after all, the girls from The Hula Palace: The U.S.O of Castro Street. We were there to party. 590 Castro was a number one ticket to fairy land.

We were free to be as exotic and erotic as we wanted to be. There would be mistakes: red wine on white satin; glitter on all the floors; clumsy, awkward men in dresses; rugged undressed men; men in full leather; oils, spices, drugs, Crisco, rubber cowboy toys in the freezer, along with rotting pudding, and unlabeled drugs. Even a weekend of hunting Easter Eggs hidden up colorful, tattooed manly asses. "Men, while never meaning to, can make awful messes, Rachel," we tried to explain. We begged her to "loosen up," "join the party," "get a grip," and "let that luscious Breck hair down, gurl!" Buy a dress for Christ's sake.

Rachel honestly didn't quite know how to loosen up. She wore a man's short-haired wig and a polyester suit when her family visited from their white castle in Palos Verdes. I always made sure I was in a housedress cleaning the hall. He would never let them up the stairs. I would go to the front bay and watch out the windows, waving as they talked at the car or go down and sweep the sidewalk.

Rachel felt we should be more Gump's girls and less Salvation Army. The die was cast, there was lipstick on the walls, and we were the Matson Line Girls and the Lone Cowboy. "Three to two, we win! Meeting adjourned."

Rachel was gone, and yes, dare I say it, her Miserable Little Dog too.

If you got to go, you got to go especially if you have been asked to!

I must say that Rachel did go on to marry European royalty and live in flawless splendor in the south of France, of course. I had pangs of grumpy guilt; after all I am not very nice and was never ever kind to her, on purpose and just for fun. She was losing The Hula Palace, and so I gave her the African Goddess bust as a going away present. She did have style—I just don't know whose. The Bitch!

Ms. Blue's departure was not far behind Rachel's. He was so hot and had an exciting huge juicy looking basket and a really cute little butt; too bad he couldn't get with the program.

Years later, in 1978, I saw him one night at the South of Market Club. We fell in lust. We slipped into a glory hole booth and made passionate animals of ourselves. He would have made a great lover. We went upstairs to the balcony for a breather and some pot. Sitting in the bleachers, I lit it up and he asked me who I was and what I did. I knew he hadn't figured it out: the sex was too hot for ordinary familiarity.

I wanted to savor this. He had been such a bastard to Etta. I raised my shoulders and moved them from side to side to shake my hairy tits. Then, in a slow, sultry voice, I said to him, breathlessly, "It's me, The Princess."

"The Princess?" he questioned.

"Yes, Darling, from the Hula Palace. It's me, ELA Lee. You know, Lee Lee. Surprise! I always wanted to fuck with you and now I have!"

The look on his face was the horror of an uptight male who doesn't sleep with drag queens. It was a look of dismay, shock, and revulsion, like he had just found a roach in his soup. I knew it: she was having a Fem Attack. He just needed a Midol to complete the picture.

Of course, she got up and left in a huff. "I love you too!" I yelled as he stormed towards the door. "Ba-Bye Sweetheart…!"

Bunny called it a grudge fuck. Miss Bette Davis would just bark, "HA!"

As for me? Well, I just treasure all my own moments.

After all, I'm a Princess!

Lee Mentley at the Krishna Festival. Photo by Daniel Nicoletta

Tibetan Princess Iory Allison.
Photo, a Selfie, by Iroy

BUS STOP

HOT Denims
Blue gene buttocks
Hit the streets
From folded Gucci bags
Screaming
Beat me ...!
Fuck me ...!
Buy me a Hamilton Beach.

In 1974 San Francisco, the #8 Market to the Castro—an electric bus or trolley as Etta liked to imagine things—would slip up congested Market Street, pedestrians weaving around it. The bus careened alongside the still in process construction of the rapid transit boondoggle named BART for Bay Area Rapid Transit, offering us above-ground glimpses of its sparkling, gritty, disemboweled caverns.

I had spent most of last night trolling for sex in the pouring rain and in the dark, wet tunnels beneath the trolleys and street racket.

I walked from the Castro to 5th Street underground in the dark. Although it was just over a mile, I could spend hours traversing this smarmy journey. I treasured the sounds of steaming echoes on dirty water and footsteps in the shadows, not knowing whose they were. I remember cobalt blue reflections on strangers' skin from artificial moonlight provided by the workmen's flickering lights.

The #8 Market would end up slinking into the Castro, turning right up 18th Street. Then it slid past the fabulous South China Cafe, just across the street from a real pig-hole joyful fag bar called The Pendulum. It turned left at Collingwood, past the recreation center connected to the Most Holy Redeemer Catholic School's playground and baseball field for the good Catholic people's little children. After school, however, this rec center, park and restrooms became the church's worst nightmare. Late at night, like most of the city streets and dark recesses, this playground—or the Collingwood Tea Room, as we preferred to call it—was swamped with late night sexual warriors looking for prey.

HRH Lee Mentley, East LA 1972. Photo by Para

The screeching #8 Market would come to the end of the line and park two and three buses deep, running the entire length of the Hula Palace at 590 Castro. The drivers would usually leave their turn signals on and, as the lights blinked, their horns would blare BLAM, BLAM, and BLAM after BLAM in a cacophony of the most irritable sounds. It was the worst torture imaginable except perhaps bamboo under my fancy nails which I kept pretty, thanks to Thursdays at I Magnin's with my sisters Goldie Glitters and Divine. Their memory burns bright!

"If one is to look this attractive and spend late nights in the clutches of endless handsome gentlemen, a gurl has to get a little rest!" I screamed from under my covers, barely awakened from my dreams. Maybe I was still dreaming? Was this Sunday? All I wanted was to languish in the lazy euphoria of slowly rising. But No …! I sought, I wanted—no, I needed—oblivion. I had to savor the memories of last night's romp. BUT NO! Those fucking electric buses blare BLAM! BLAM! BLAM! Honestly, I'd have killed them all if I wasn't such a fucking pacifist. Honestly, the only thing I want to shoot is orgasms! BLAM!

Dear Goddess, please! Where's my life going? BLAM! Oh, my head! I'm being dragged up to the surface of reality by the #8. BLAM! And with no caffeine! BLAM! Too much bright light! BLAM! Rude awakening from the Princess' dream state wasn't a pretty picture. BLAM! I thought I was allowed to have as much sex as I wanted and no one would disturb me! BLAM! Oh please don't let this be Sunday! BLAM!

The new girls downstairs were hanging out their windows screaming at the bus drivers. BLAM! The drivers had walked across the street to the New Diamond Market for their coffee breaks with callous disregard for the sleep of us poor humble women. BLAM!

I dragged myself out of bed and slipped into my silky red kimono with the gold braid. BLAM! I love the feel of silk on my waist and thighs and how the braid rubbed against my hairy breasts making them perky and rise to the occasion. I have always believed that lounging well is the best revenge and I gave it my best here! BLAM! Did it feel good ... ? OUCH ... ! My poor tits were so sore from last night. That damn Jeffery—a sweet boyfriend I'd had for ten years, who actually bought the brass bed from Etta we'd spent our first 3 days in together—always wore me raw!

BLAM! I staggered into the kitchen where I tried to focus on anything tangible and grounding. BLAM! There in the dish drain were last night's dishes. BLAM! I flung them out the open window on to the street. BLAM! They hit with a smashing success, multi-colored pottery shards everywhere! BLAM! I leaned out the window and saw the girls on the second floor below looking up at me in startled amazement. BLAM!

"Hi Girrllls...!" BLAM!

I waved. BLAM! They had only just moved in and had no real idea what it would take to get the drivers' attention. BLAM! How could they? Besides they were real girls (in a biological way) who didn't even have the good sense to wear bracelets or make-up! BLAM! They didn't know how to make big gurrlll noise yet. We had a much better sense of the feminine than they did with their butched-up 1960s ways. I'll have to give lessons! BLAM!

What could they know? BLAM! Straight boys, that's what. Soon there would be straight boys. I shouted operatically out the kitchen window and, in a Loretta Young twirl of my kimono, I did a little naughty hula. BLAM! Soon there would be straight boys! BLAM! Two drinks, that's what it takes two drinks! Soon there would be straight boys. "Hi, Dolls!" I waved again. This was so much fun! BLAM!

The blinkers were still blaring. BLAM! BLAM! So I shut the window and tried to figure out how I could get a cup of coffee without breaking my nails. BLAM! I sank down into the Mexican blue kitchen chair, hoping I could just be Low Key, my Chinese drag queen persona, for the rest of the day. BLAM! Maybe I should have some of Etta's chamomile tea? BLAM! With half a Quaalude—aka, disco biscuits.

Just then, I heard the door slam and someone very animated running up the steps. What Now? It had to be Jimbo, aka Ms. Gumm, my dear lovely clumsy sister, college lover, and nephew of Judy herself, but mostly a some-

Bus Stop Princess, Lady Diana, Neon Maroon. Photo, by Pérez

what endearing nuisance. Jimbo was out for her sixth or seventh try at jumping off the bridge. At my encouragement, I may add, I gave him the 75 cent fare to the bridge, any bridge last night in order to get rid of him. That was Saturday … I think? Is this Sunday? Confusion about time and place ruled The Hula Palace.

Gurrlll, get a grip. I just couldn't take it anymore. Bitch, bitch, bitch, that's all she does. If I had half his talent I would have been a Nuevo York social success and have done Carnegie Hall by now. I had to dare him to jump. I'm so sick of his blues. I knew he wouldn't do it. She always threatens to jump but he never does. At least when our lovely Miss Clayton jumped he took an appropriate amount of LSD with several Quaaludes and really got into the jump as an adventure. So of course she lived; he even made the cover of San Francisco Magazine. In the end, she was a Star. "A Really Big Star", as Tahara would say!

At first The Hula Palace was concerned about Jimbo but by now we had his number and most of us just wanted him to jump. He was horribly fixated on his late great aunt, the infamous Ms. Judy Gumm Garland. For Jimbo, everything was a little bit over the rainbow. As my young green-eyed college lover I found him a rascal and radically romantic. Very Sexy. But now, like Liza's character Pookie Adams, in The Sterile Cuckoo, he just irritated me. The thrill was gone. What can I say ...? This wasn't Kansas, I had no red heels, and it wasn't turning into a good day.

I looked up. "Oh dear!" He was ecstatic over finding a small, white-flecked Christmas pine tree decorated with little red bows and gold balls. I could see him through the reflection of the stained glass on the salon door. He was showing it to Ms. Maggie known as Neon Maroon an Italian bomb shell from Hollywood with eggplant colored hair who had also just entered the dining salon. She walked toward me. "He chose this over suicide?" she said, pointing to the Christmas tree. "Maybe I'm the one who should jump."

"Maybe we should all jump."

It was late February, almost March. Where does he find all this shit he drags home? His room looks like the Goodwill free box. I was speechless. Pérez entered the kitchen clutching her head. She saw Jimbo's tree and for a moment she thought her hangover was so bad she had completely missed Christmas.

"Did we wake you, darling?"

I politely asked her to open the window. I was feeling faint and needed a lot of air. As she pulled up the large Victorian window, BLAM! The blaring of the #8's signals grabbed my brain again. BLAM! I turned to Jimbo. I could only focus on his cute little tree. BLAM! It was making me sick. I took her little tree from him. BLAM! I walked over to the window. BLAM!

My lesbian Gumm-ball sister screamed "Give me that tree, that's my tree!"

BLAM! He grabbed it back. BLAM!

"Ms. Gumm. Give me that tree!" BLAM!

"No!" BLAM!

"I love that tree!"

BLAM!

"Ms. Gumm. Give me that tree!"

"No!"

BLAM!

"This is the Princess talking, darling. You wouldn't like me to take you out for a walk on the bridge, myself?" BLAM! "Would you, my pretty?" BLAM!

He handed the miserable, dried, white-flecked orphan tree over to me. BLAM! I turned. BLAM! And without looking I threw it out of the window! BLAM! Leaning out and clutching my bosom and flouncing kimono, I watched the white-flecked dead tree as it neatly landed, standing straight up next to the rude driver who was sucking his puke coffee through his greedy nasty lips. BLAM!

Astonished, the driver looked up. I waved my electric blue fan screaming "Merry Fucking Christmas, you loud mother fucker!" BLAM! "Turn those fuckin' blares off …!" BLAM!

He gave me the finger and screamed some bloody obscenity. BLAM! How dare he respond to the Princess in any fashion? This penetrated my nerves. BLAM! I'll get this little bastard! I'll twist his little tits till they look like cows udders! BLAM!

I slammed the window shut and went to the phone to call MUNI. I asked for the Municipal Transportation Complaint Desk. "You know, the one for those provincial little green buses that are so loved by fucking tourists," I told the operator. She transferred my call. I read all the beads I could muster till I climbed the paper pusher's trail and got to the head queen in charge. I told that head queen on the other end of the line that sometime soon the entire building on 19th and Castro was going to collapse and crush one of her #8 Market Neanderthals, just from the weight of the anger of the Princess of Castro Street!

She really worked my nerves with his official jargon. I eventually screamed that "this is why I needed my sleep!" I slammed down the phone. Pérez looked at me and said "I'll be right back." The smell of timid bureaucratic power sickens me. The faint sound of the horn blares could still be heard as the #8 turned the corner and headed back into the city.

I walked over to Ms. Gumm and held him in my arms. We mourned the passing of her poor little tree. I asked her why he hadn't jumped. She just fluttered his beautiful sad green eyes at me and joyfully tapped off down the hall into the front salon whimsically singing "I want to live! I want to live!" and "I've got to be me!"

"That Bad Gurrlll? You'll wake Etta, Ms. Gumm." I slide over to the window. I sat down and held my head in my hands. Pérez came back into the room with some fresh Bloody Mary's and a joint in her gills. The smell of tabasco and vodka put a smile back on my face. Even if it was only a smirk, she always managed to put a grin on my face.

"The blares have stopped," she noted. "Light that joint Princess."

Etta emerged from her Vaseline vault. "What's all the racket, gurls?"

She sauntered into the kitchen in his baby blue pastel golden dragon lady nightwear. He looked around at the four of us and sighed. "Princess, you got in late last night. In the tunnels again, ELA Lee, darling?" She shook his finger at me, as she often did. "Where's Robert?"

"He's over at Tom Smith's house, his new hunky biker buddy, up on 18th."

"Where did he meet this one?"

"At the clinic, HA!"

"That Boy!"

Etta went over to the sink to get her special little tea cup. She looked at the empty sink and the empty counter. He turned and looked at me. "Lee Lee, darling, did you throw the dishes out the window again?" We all laughed.

"Etta, would I do a thing like that? No, I actually threw a tree."

She came over to me, shaking that finger in my face. "It's Sunday, you asshole. We are having lots of boys over for dinner tonight, ELA, and you threw out the dishes! That's not nice, Princess. I promised I would twist those hairy tits if you did this again!"

Etta came at me. "No! Not the tits! ETTA! ETTA! GIRRLLL FIGHT! GIRL FIGHT!"

All I wanted was to go back to bed. "Not the tits, they hurt! Stop it Etta! Is it really Sunday? Yes, Etta, Ok! Ok! I'm sorry. Really, I am. I couldn't take it anymore Etta. The trolley was blaring. Yes, I threw the dishes at the driver and the little tree too. I'm sorry, sweetheart. What can I do to make it up to you?" Etta gives me such a look that I wonder if he'll buy the little baby LeRoy act or not. "Ok Etta, please forgive me, what can I do?"

She just continued looking at me with that indignant Etta look. Then, she throws up her hands into the air and proclaims: "At Princess ELA's expense we will all go shopping for new dinnerware after brunch."

"Yay!" Neon and Pérez yelled.

We love to go thrift shopping. But what to wear ... Suddenly, we are all Gay again!

* * * * *

It wasn't long before the city changed the #8

HRH Lee Mentley. Paintng by Michael Shain 1973

Market route. They began to stop across the street in front of New Diamond Market. But would this stop you ...? It didn't stop us ...! They continued to blare their horn blinkers and we were always buying more dishes. We never ran away from a fight.

All of this was perfectly wonderful because nothing is wonderfully perfect. After all, even little wars are about sex and sexism! Yes, we would have to go shopping now because I had a little bitch fight with an inconsiderate bus driver, but honestly there was a much more ominous, big boy war brewing in Texas, something deadlier than noisy busses. Tonight we would have a special Soup Kitchen to welcome the new American refugees from the Lone Star state.

What they don't tell you about the Lone Star state is that it's overflowing with mindless idiots. Texas isn't the "Wild West"—it's just Home for the Paranoid. Ap-

42

parently, from all the recent dish on the streets, there had been a horrific mass murder committed by some deranged pedophiles in Texas. Wretched, loathsome pedophiles that lured, seduced and then murdered a large number of young male hitchhikers. Once their grizzly deeds were uncovered, there was a spontaneous mass hysteria directed toward homosexuals in general.

The national media didn't help any by labeling these attacks as "Gay Murders"—as though murder could be "gay." The sensationalism and subsequent attacks on our community instigated a mass pilgrimage of young Texans who had become the victims of these irrational hate crimes. Many naive, innocent young men were pouring into the Castro looking for a safer life. It seemed that the small minds in the big state of Texas couldn't differentiate between the affections of young bucks for male companionship from the insane crimes of mass murderers.

We started these Sunday soup kitchens for stranded local artists and runaways, but now we had refugees from the Bible Belt as well. We tried to help them get back in touch with their families, seeing if we could send them back to mommy and daddy. Sadly, that didn't happen all that often, so at best we could help them get food stamps for a while, and maybe a job washing dishes, busing and waiting on tables. San Francisco was Wonderland and suddenly everyone wanted to be an Alice, and somehow at the Hula Palace we'd become the City's White Rabbit.

Brunch was scrumptious. A perfect veggie omelet including Ms. Pérez's extra special hot salsa and Spanish cut home-fried potatoes. Once my Bloody Mary was refreshed I forgot all about the nasty bus driver and being Low Key. I wanted to hit the streets and go shopping!

"OK! GIRRLLLS! The bus to the Mission leaves in 20 minutes so get your shopping gear on!" We went through our wardrobes, then through each other's. Two hours later, we left bedecked as the Little Rascals. I wore my Mickey Mouse tee-shirt, Neon was Tinker Bell, Pérez was in one of my Sophia Loren dresses, and Etta dressed as Gandhi.

TAXI!

We piled out at the Purple Heart Thrift Store on Mission Street near the old stone Armory. We would start here and work our way over to Sally Ann's and maybe Saint Vincent's before we refreshed our shopped-out brains with the Goddess Artista's caffeine at Hamburger Mary's. After that, we could taxi home with our booty.

"Oh, look in the window: there's more Fiestaware!" Neon pointed out.

"Get it all," I exclaimed. I charged through the door straight for the back wall to hunt for decent plates and bowls for tonight's soup kitchen festivities. Etta went looking for a new tea cup. Pérez really never knew where to look and ended up in the drapery section—but then again, she will wear anything. We even put a rug on her one night and brought her to the Stud. She ended up on somebody's floor, no doubt!

"I may have to have a new hat," I was thinking when I noticed that the people working in the back were throwing boxes of stuff into their dumpster. "We'll just have to check out the alley on our way east."

I spotted a whole stack of Tepco plates. I turned to see who I could notice to deliver the good news that we wouldn't have to eat off of paper or Melmac tonight. I saw Etta, she looked up, and I held up my finds and described them. "Look! A great collection of old 50s drive-in diner plates with a slightly raised rim, frosted in green, pink, blue and a soft gold. You like them?" She nodded. Mission complete—time to buy hats!

Purple Heart had the best silk rayon dresses and Hawaiian shirts in town. Our collective collection at the Hula Palace had to number at least two hundred Matson Line shirts and many, many more dresses. They also had those old pure cotton grandma kitchen table cloths with sweet little scenes of ducks, the countryside, cherries, or Mexican motifs. Those made excellent head-wraps and wrap-around skirts over my Levis. When I was in the Islands, it was all I wore. You couldn't have too many. Neon was rapidly going through the children's section. She was barely 90 pounds and looked ever so cute in baby clothing. Little did she know that one day soon she would be in the Beverly Hills jail for skeet shooting inside a condominium she shared with her new boyfriend Donovan, such a star fucker!

Pérez was a different story. She was in the adult section fishing for what new outfit might catch her evening's conquest. The Boys from Texas won't stand a chance. For her, it will be like shooting fish in a barrel. Yes, some of the boys slept over—although sometimes they would sleep with our Hula Palace real girls and we would call them "lesbians," male lesbians and shemales.

I could see Etta making her way up to the glass cabinets. I suppose she was looking for a Buddha icon or a small bric-a-brac find. She usually found one treasure or another that would fetch a pretty penny in another store. She had an eye for under-appraised items, especially ones she could slip into her satin corset or pants pocket on the sly.

"Trading up, Etta?" I bumped her hip to make her notice the new 1920s crown I had found. "Like it, Etta?"

"It's you, Princess!" It was burgundy, velvet, and had black egret feathers and it was only 45 cents!

By the time we fled the musty smell of the secondhand store to explore the box of free items in the alley behind the shop—where, incidentally, we found cartons of goodies to give away to the boys on the street—we were exhausted. We never even made it to the other thrift shops or Mary's to see Artista. We taxied back to the Castro, dropped the loot off with Neon at the laundry to purify it from any possible lice for the comfort of our guests. I dropped Etta and The Pérez at the Hula Palace, and then had the taxi drop me at Cala Foods to do the shopping. Boy, could we stretch a buck.

I was working at The Haven, an organic cafe across from the magnificent City of Paris department store downtown off Union Square. I had convinced management to hire three of Cockettes: Pristine Condition dressed as Betty Crockett, Etta as a Carrot, and Candy or sometimes Billy Orchid as Alice's Mushroom, all designed by the Fabulous Joseph. They wandered Union Square and the downtown business district scaring tourists and passing out flyers for our famous seven-grain bread orgasmic sandwiches.

At the end of the day I took home all the leftover vegetables and bread that would otherwise end up trashed or secretly shared with the Downtown homeless. So while living with five roommates to keep the rent down—after all it was $185 a month for a lousy fourteen rooms—we could still eat like royalty, albeit out of the trash. It was Divinely Decadent—thank you, Mr. Isherwood, for I was Sally Bowles in another life or maybe just last week. All we really had to shop for was butter, milk, rice, pinto beans, tortillas, Etta's lentils, and maybe a blonde or two for dessert. Everything else we had delivered.

I walked home and from the top of the landing, the moment I opened the door I could smell the spicy, savory cooking of Etta and Pérez. Somehow the odors were always somewhere between Mexico and an English forest home of a Gay Robin Hood. I walked into the kitchen. "The quickest way to a man's heart, they say." "We know," came the chorus.

"Smells good, Etta. Here's the rest." I put the bag into her arms. "I have got to freshen up, darlings, and lie down for a bit. Call me when it is ready."

"OK, Princess."

"This has been quite a day," I said to myself as I slipped into a hot shower. The pounding water felt good on my sore but sensuous body. I loved the rushing of water and its erotic implications. I dried off and slipped into my Air Force jumpsuit. I went into Robert's room and spread out on the waterbed. I had wild dreams of men battling over rooms in a house that was forever growing. In my dream, I couldn't understand why they were warring over what was readily available to them everywhere. The hall grew and grew and the doors expanded and expanded as the rooms multiplied. I could hear noises of clomping feet and voices like coyotes crying in a desert.

As I woke, feeling like I was suffocating, I realized that the guests were arriving. Sometimes there would be as many as 50. By breakfast there would still be about 20. Sometimes I would just leave and sleep outside on the street because the Hula Palace was too full. On the other hand, how can you have too many men? I must be losing my mind. What would tonight bring?

Jim Gumm at The Haven Union Square.
Photo by Pérez 1973

I gathered what was left of my butch self and sauntered down the hall to the top of the stairs. "OK girl, pull it together. You can do it," I said to myself. I glanced over at the giant Playbill of Mona Mandrake and Ruth Weiss at the Spaghetti Factory in North Beach that hung over the stairway and took a deep breath. "If war-torn Mona Mandrake having survived the blitz could face the world after all she has been through with degenerate men, I guess I can, too." I proceeded to greet the white boys from the south.

It was with a profound sense of sorrow that I met the young men who were coming to seek the Gay Dream. Here they are, these lovely young men, cast out on to the streets that have no real gold unless you sell your special parts to a guilty queen, who was herself once a dejected youth cruising the streets years before. It was distressing how mean-spirited humans can be to each other. These kids needed help and it was going to take more than a bowl of soup, a free box—the kind San Franciscans use to give things away —and address of the General Assistance Office to receive some very generous welfare money to get them stated. I would have to talk to Harvey about all this. He was our unofficial fairy mayor and, though none of us would have believed it, soon to be our elected supervisor—an absurdly high office for a queer hippie camera shop owner. Maybe he does have a plan? He promised me he does.

The boys were all assembled in the kitchen and parlor. When I let the last of them in, I walked into the chaos of a feeding frenzy. Etta, seeing the dismay on my face, announced "The Princess has arrived."

"OK, Boys, take a seat, and listen up. We don't do this for our health so pay attention or we might throw you out. We have a little custom here at the Hula Palace. Starting with the handsome young man here on my right we are going to introduce ourselves and say where we are from. We will do our best to help you get established here in Oz and we will help you if you want to get reconnected with your family. Okay, boy—what's your name?"

"My name is Carl, I'm from Cisco, Texas. My father threw me out when he found out I was queer. I came here hoping to start a new life and find a job."

"Good to meet you, Carl. Next?"

"I'm Hank, from Dallas. My lover John and I left because of all the violence over the murders. We got beaten up pretty bad outside the High Country dance bar in Cedar Springs. Our families didn't understand why we were there together. When they found out they threatened to beat us too. So we left. We would like to open a small business and have a new life."

"Sorry to hear that Hank. You and John will be safe here and we will do what we can. It's good to know you have a plan!"

"You have to be careful here on the streets, too," I continued. "Just ask Neon. She was attacked last week and called a fag. She was pissed off because for one she is a real girl and second she has marched many times with us all to City Hall for Harvey and thought she was safe. Never make that mistake, there are good and bad people everywhere, including San Francisco."

Etta looked across at me. We have heard all this before. The next boy I had seen on the streets all week. A real looker, I had hoped he would come. He was tall and lanky, a 60s hippy heart throb. His long dark hair and soft blue eyes gave him an air of wisdom beyond his years.

"Howdy, my name is Star Blanket I am part American Indian, Japanese and German. I come from a very mixed background. I was raised by my Cherokee grandmother after my mom and dad died in a car accident and then she passed on when I was 15. So I moved in with my German uncle in El Paso. He wanted to have sex with me all the time, so I ran away. For over a year, I have been hitchhiking around the states ever since, and now I finally made it to Frisco. I hadn't heard about the trouble back home in Texas until now and I am sure glad I'm not there. I heard about your soup kitchen and can't pass up a free meal, sir."

"That's 'San Francisco' not 'Frisco,' Star Blanket, and at home they call me 'The Princess.' Later at night I'm called 'Sir' or 'Master Bastard' if you dare."

They all laughed! One by one around the table, we listened to the sad and terrible tales of life at home in the U. S. of A. wastelands.

Another boy I'd like to meet later in the tunnels was named Dean, a mechanic from Ohio. He had made it out here with the money he saved by taking old heaps and transforming them into workable cars. He was hoping to set up his own classical car restoration shop over in the Fell Street area. I even offered to do his inventory for him. I have lots of fantasies about garages and greasy hands.

I reminded them that if they wanted to call home they could use the phone but because of the expense they had to limit their talking to a few minutes. If they wanted to stay and set down roots, they could use the address of the Hula Palace as their place of residence. This way they could get Food Stamps and some General Assistance from the government. I was told by Linda at the Department of Social Services that when she punched out our address on the computer it was over 12 pages long. I let them know if they needed references for applications to go ahead and use our names and we could supply them with others who would help, too. They just had to keep us up to date on their plans so we didn't get our wires crossed.

Dinner proceeded like the miracle of the loaves and fishes. I will never understand where Etta got all the food but somehow everyone got to eat as much as they wanted. We once again had to hear about how the mass murders happened and all the other gay bashing going on because of this Christian Texan hysteria. Fortunately, these are details I cannot remember.

"You know, gentlemen and ladies that nowhere in the great Bible is the word 'Homosexual' mentioned. In the scriptures that pseudo-Christians most like to mention, there are only references to an ancient law about temple prostitutes and to the sins of Sodom which were, according to the Bible, apparently being inhospitable to God's angels. And, I must say that at the Hula Palace, we are never disrespectful to angels! You're our angels tonight.

Welcome to San Francisco and The Hula Palace!"

"The Princess always has to have something poetic to say, doesn't she?" Pérez retorts.

"What was the question, Pérez? Or are you just jealous because your mouthy talents lie in another direction and have so few words of wisdom to spit up for anyone? Just look at her knees! Go ahead, Hank. They have dents in them; she's had pads sewn on to cover up the scars."

"Always the bitch, Princess."

"Always aware, darling, of sex kitten games when I see them."

"You really think you are royalty, don't you, fag?"

"Did I say something funny, darling? Something crusty to offend you, my sweet?"

"No, just your usual drivel." Her orneriness meant she clearly needed dick.

"I love it when you talk butch to me! That's why they call me 'The Princess' and you darling, 'The Help!'"

And with that remark, I realize it's time for me to leave. I want to hit the streets before we start demolishing the new dinnerware.

Obviously Pérez's Quaalude had worn off. "Take some more drugs, girlfriend, and maybe someone here will sleep with you. Star Blanket did. He found both of us to his sweet liking! I thank you for the company boys and the fine cooking, Etta. And, of course, thank you again, Ms. Pérez, for being, well, you."

I turned to Etta and suggested the boys wash the dishes and reminded her that they best be in the pantry when I return and not readily available for me to toss out the window in the morning. I really couldn't afford this disposable lifestyle anymore along with all the party drugs we needed to keep us going.

I stood at the foot of the Palace stairs breathing in the cool City air at 19th and Castro. Which way will the wind blow me tonight? Do I want a cowboy, a rock star, or someone from under the shadows? I started walking down Castro toward 18th.

I took in the lights of The Castro Theater marquee. I am a rainbow-colored creature of dark shadows. It must be in my Italian Gypsy blood. I needed the mystery of the streets and the secrets of yet unknown men. Who will he be tonight? What would be his dreams? What would he want me to do? What would I do to him? What was my need? It was a wet, cold, musty night.

49

Alongside the brightly hued lights teeming through the thick clumps of luminous fog, I could smell the sweet sweat wafting from the bars. I walked toward windy Market Street and headed off into the fray.

As I passed Anderson Hardware I started to think it was too cold and maybe I don't want to be out here right now and started back down Castro. I crossed over the intersection to Hibernia Bank and up across 18th into the corner store. I thought I would buy some ice cream or pie and bring it back to The Palace for desert and try to lay Dean and talk about cars. There's no pie to be had, so I picked up two gallons of chocolate and one vanilla and started walking back toward home.

As I stepped up on to the curb, a drunk flew out of the Midnight Sun. The door man, Fuck Me Patty, screamed after him. I turned to the outside of the walkway and noticed a limousine slink around the corner. The back window slid down and the handsome romantic man within asked if the Air Force needed a ride? He was referring to my clever jumpsuit outfit, although the fact that I was bearded made it pretty obvious I was not an enlisted man; clearly, we were both interested in playing out some fantasies. I looked again and said, "Are you talking to me?"

"You want a ride"?

I looked again. "Are you who I think you are"?

"Who do you think I am?"

I knew exactly who he was! I turned to the next queen who stepped up on the curb and handed him the brown paper bag, saying "Here's your dessert." I hastily climbed into the posh leather of the dark limousine, and wrapped my arms around the incognito, adorable blonde superstar, someone who obviously needed an Air Force daddy to show him the sights.

We cruised through the back streets then out over the Golden Gate Bridge for hours in what seemed like suspended animation, shared some down home kissing, lovemaking, and promises of roses in the morning. I told him my name was "Steve" and that I had just gotten into town from Twentynine Palms where I was stationed. I told him I had grown up in San Francisco. I said that I always took my leave here in the city, so I could meet guys and not have to worry about being found out at the base.

I told him I had spent a lot of time cruising sailors as a teenager at The Pike, an amusement park in Long Beach. The first time I went there with my family on summer vacation, I discovered my first glory hole and sexy graffiti, including a brightly painted flying phallus with white wings and a very pink dick.

I told him I had stolen my first car within a week of seeing the glory hole and hit the park by myself. I told him I had never gotten over my first blow job through a glory hole. I have always needed to repeat and repeat the experience. He said "Here, look" as he cut a hole in a piece of stiff paper. He loved this rap.

What an amazing night! As my mother Sarah always said about a good time and a good man—usually meaning her favorite musicians, Gene Autry or Buck Owens—"He can put his boots and guitar under my bed anytime." We returned over Golden Gate Bridge and once again, under a fake identity, I made deep passionate love to my own musical stranger. Sometimes I live my life "like a candle in the wind".

Hours later, after seeing the lights of San Francisco from so many positions, and in an air of satisfied contentment, he dropped me back off at Market and Castro. I slowly stretched

John Serrian. Photo by Pérez

out of the limo-dream and began the walk down into the village. There were a lot of men on the street. Events in Texas had filled the street with a new dimension: cowboys and corn-fed sweethearts from the Fly Over states.

It just wasn't Texas either, something was happening. Men, boys, queens, gurls, real girrlls, shemales, and lesbians too, were showing up from everywhere and we knew it was becoming an increasingly problematic situation. Harvey Milk, who was politically more mature than the rest of us, was organizing as quickly as he could. Too many people were coming into the community. This would become a problem we'd have to face sooner or later. Harvey hoped we would be ready when the big boys of Texas and America's right wing wanted to have a political showdown in San Francisco. Harvey knew how to move political power from his anti-war views. Somehow we trusted this boastful queen from New York to know what was right.

I myself had seen something like this before in the Haight Ashbury, and in Silver Lake near Griffith Park in Los Angeles, during the turbulent 60s. Artists find a depressed community and move in. Everybody follows in line because of all the excitement and freshness of spirit. Economic interest grows and speculators nose around until boom time is certain before they buy in. Then the artists who won't sell out are forced out, then somehow a publicist born in hell invites the mega-culture. They label the "quaint" art community "a shopping area." Some civil rights, would-be-chic, rip-off groups move into what's now called "The Village." And then, a frightening political movement that puts Americans to shame is born. The money people call what remains "artsy" and "progressive." They sell tee-shirts, appropriate bric-a-brac, and push bad drugs and greedy attitudes.

Believe me, it's not like living from a place of passion or truth. These sorts of people will exchange everything for money. The venture capitalists attempt to show us how to live and what to think. They give us the "truth" of what life is really all about: looking good in sex, power and real estate—and, of course, fuck humanity and embrace nothing truly gay. This is the essence of the new Gayourgeoisie.

In any case, these men were growing more and more gorgeous, and increasingly aware that they were as hot as everyone thought they were. There seemed to be more posing on the street, more boots, more swarthy leather dudes sitting on bikes and on hoods of cars. There was a prevalent Ivy League crowd, with brown leather desire to meet Mr. Right. Very "let's move in and set up house," perpetuating the whole Ozzie and Harriet Nelson (or in this case "Ricky and Ricky Nelson") homo-syndrome. I love the butch look, but I hate the Norman Rockwell look: tacky chandeliers and perfumed, pastel-colored soap balls. Where have these people been shopping? At a 60s mall, I'm afraid. What's next? Leisure suits? Gay golfers?

I walked quickly through the gauntlet of rubber daddies and hysterical Janes (the kind of girl who plays strip poker in high school and gets so flummoxed when an Elvis or a James Dean type comes around that you just want to slap her and shut her nasty ass up.) I walked straight past The Midnight Sun and proceeded up the slope to the Hula Palace. As I passed Tommy's Plants and then the Arab liquor store, I noticed there was someone standing in the shadow of the Hula Palace stairwell. It was Wayne Quinn, Upper Market Street Gallery artist extraordinaire, an exhibitor at the Hula Palace Salons and, I guess, the queen of the late night stoops. I was about to call out to her, as any gay gurl would, noticing a sister cruising in the dark of her own home.

Just then, I noticed a group of young thugs running down the hill from 20th Street. They had a baseball bat, a dog and were screaming obscenities about fags and headed toward Wayne. He seemed oblivious to their onslaught. I started running toward 590, yelling for Wayne to climb up the stairs. He finally heard me yell, but rather than retreating inside, stupidly came out on to the sidewalk to see what I was saying.

When he finally turned around, they were almost upon him. He ran as fast as he could for the stairs and climbed them as I passed by him. I screamed at the bastards, yelling that if they came any closer, I would rip out their fucking throats with my bare hands and kill their fucking dog! "Come On You Mother Fuckers! I'm going to make your asses bleed. I'll kill your sweet young tight asses and stuff you up your dog's ass!"

I could see that this was not the reaction they expected, so it threw them totally off guard. After all, these boys usually come down here to beat up sissies. It's rare for them to find men who will kick their anxious, itchy, deprived little butts back to the suburbs, the Mission and the Sunset District, back home to their homophobic daddies.

I remember one time when a carload of white boys from Daily City started harassing queers on Castro Street from inside their vehicle. They kept it up, circling the block a few times. They would turn right on 18th, right onto Noe Street, right at 19th, and then right back down Castro. This brought them right in front of Castro Camera where Harvey Milk lived. I noticed their pattern from the turret of the front salon at the Hula Palace. I called Harvey on the phone.

He said, "Meet me on the street." I grabbed my brass flute—one that was 14 or 16 inches long and which I played for real and often had up the sleeve of my leather jacket—and ran down the stairs. I crossed the street. As I got there, they were coming around again. They were screaming "Fag" and "Suck my dick, fag" as I ran across to the front of the Castro Camera. Harvey rushed out of the door with his baseball bat, barely clothed. He jumped on the back of the car. I, of course, followed. We started beating on the windows and hitting the car roof.

Those boys didn't know how to handle this new perspective on fags and sissies. They made their big mistake by turning left on 18th where all the boys were cruising. The gay boys had witnessed the little romp of these white boys going around the block. They encircled the car and started shaking it until the children inside completely cracked and started crying like the babes they were. Harvey had them arrested.

I loved Harvey. I bet the blonde driver boy got it from his dad, and badly, when he got home. Turns out his dad was a cop. Honestly, they should have let me spank them; I could have made it fun and shared my whole Master Bastard persona with them!

Anyway, the boys on the hill tonight, still stunned from my no-holds-barred verbal defense, turned around and headed back up away from The Hula Palace. The Princess and her little tirade had frightened them again! Wayne sneaked back down the stairs just so he could witness some of my performance.

I stood there with my hands on my hips, catching my breath. He looked at me in astonishment at the little verbal exchange I had with the punks. He mentioned that I may have saved his life.

I took a deep breath, "I guess I probably did, dear. This has been one rough Sunday. You'll have to excuse me, Wayne, but I need to crawl up the stairs and collapse."

"Oh, and Wayne," I continued, "pay attention out here next time. Keep your eyes and ears open. If you can't fight, you should carry a gun. Or better yet, just stay home if you can't handle the streets."

Just like a slightly hairier Scarlett O'Hara, I muttered to myself, "Tomorrow is another day," and climbed the sagging stairs of the Hula Palace.

Lee Mentley Performing At MOMA
Horse head created by Nickolus Kauainos
Photo by Pérez

HULA AT NIGHT

Silence
No words
One night only one
To be there holding you
To clutch and cling
Just holding on to you
Pure love
Lying in bed
Both are silent
Nothing said.

*E*ttalinda Carne had a fantasy of being gleefully taken by a big, tough—as she would say, a "Mandingo Man"—while she wore a pink hoop skirt. So Pola the demure, Shirley our lady of the night, ELA the "hair-suit" princess and Bunny Honey decided to slip Etta some MDA and take her to The Folsom Street Barracks for a sexual escapade.

The Barracks had a murky history. Some said it was originally the New Forester, although others claimed it was actually the Old Globe Hotel above the Red Star Saloon, a bar known for its degenerative artistry in sexual exploration and leather heavy dudes. Slowly, then all at once, the popularity of the erotic saloon spilled over into the cheap hotel, whatever it had been named. It became the vortex of San Francisco's sexual warriors and we gurls knew there would be someone there who would fulfill Etta's every wish.

She'll kill me for telling this story! In fact, when Etta realized I was about to write a tell-all she threatened to share a story about me sweeping out the trash on to Castro Street into the gutter early one morning in my 50s crinoline see-through

house dress when a certain young prince took a fancy to my Italian thighs. "Remember how he magically maneuvered you into all sorts of interesting vignettes in front of my mirror, Princess? I can tell stories, too!" she threatened.

"So what," I told her. "I loved that dress." Etta lives in a state of constant amazement at how free I am with my mouth. She tells me how pushy I could be. I say, "Welcome to the surreal world!" She started writing murder

Lee Mentley and Sparky at the Hula Palace circa 1976.
Photo by Daniel Nicoletta

mysteries where I kill my tricks and then hide them in free box costumes out in plain sight. GAWD, I love her!

"We know the perfect prince for you," I said. "Come on, Sweetheart! You can lie in your bed and dream if you want and maintain your `Pristine Condition'. But believe me; it's more fun to hang from a wall in a dark, dingy, hotel room. Just ask Shirley." The first time they tied her up, he wouldn't let them take her down for weeks. Hell, the first time I went to The Barracks myself, I ended up staying for six weeks!

We all laughed. "Oh, come on, Etta—Let's go to the baths! Just take this white pill. It will make it easier, gurrllll," I cajoled as I gave him a #740 lude.

We called a taxi. Shirley, Ann and I piled in dragging Etta along as we started popping different colored drugs that would hit as we got our lockers and/or found our rooms. Give or take a blow job, Pola and Bunny would meet us later. Ms. Pérez wanted to join in but we reminded her that no biological women were allowed in The Barracks.

At this time in the life of HRH The Princess I was into MDA with Quaaludes taken in massive quantities, along with lots of brandy in very black coffee. I honestly don't know how I survived that recipe. Why was I doing all this? I was fighting the sexual revolution on all fronts and the only way to do that was to have sex! I am a Free Man who is a Sexual Warrior!

I was obsessed with the men I saw everywhere. The good news was they were ALL avalable. Thus, I would have them all: one at a time, in groups, behind trees, in the tunnels, show room floors, parking lots, the market—wherever they were, I was ready. Who could choose? And why would you want to? All men have their special little mysteries. After all, I firmly believe men should have as many sexual experiences as they want to have, in any way, and anywhere they want to have them! I still do. Sex is a sport.

Of course one should listen to Dorothy Parker and not scare her horses. Who needs a mess?

Tonight I would add my pretty full-skirted, tangerine Shelley Winters peignoir and silver rubber butcher knife, in tribute to that cult classic film, What's the Matter with Helen?

"Use your imagination Etta, that's what it's for," I taunted as I handed her a key to room #326, the one with the farm-boy brass bed next to the window. I told her that she hadn't looked this good since the Hula Palace Annual Memorial Ann Margaret Bike Run up on Mt. Tam!

Then I wrote the words "Blood in Room #321" on the first floor locker room blackboard, put on my blonde wig went upstairs, sat down on the edge of the bed with the door open, intermittently screaming, "What's the matter with Helen?" and, in my best street pidgin, "I got the moves, baby, if you got the notion!"

And yet … no replies …

Normally, I would wear butch drag at night, i.e., leather—or nothing at all—in order to have more opportunities, but somehow Etta's fantasy of hoop skirts and big black men had sparked the hysterical side of my insatiable libido. Would someone walk by and understand just what I needed or would they all cower before the drag? I wanted to know if there was a real man in the house or not. I cried out again. I waited for what seemed like hours. There must have been a problem with my make-up or maybe the entire look was a total miscalculation.

Then, outside my door, I heard a loud commotion. I cowered for a second hoping it would be My Man about to burst in. When I rushed to the door, instead I saw "She Who Was Fish," Ms. Pérez the Merwoman, being escorted by an irate queen. She saw me and yelled, "I have a telegram for Etta!" I noticed she wore a window frame

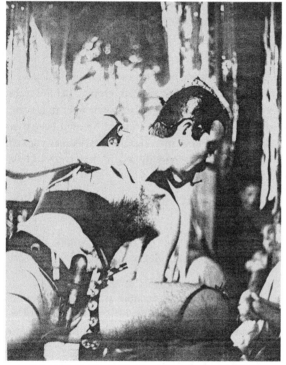

neatly displayed over her shoulder. She had actually tried to disguise herself as a window. How truly gay! Such a fashion adventuress, trying to prove she could literally wear anything!

She held out the telegram for me to grab as the House Queen dragged her past me. He was screaming bloody indignation about an actual woman breaking into the third floor. Meanwhile, she gave some old-timer a fright when she busted through the glass window on the fire escape and jumped into his private room at the end of the hall, just to deliver a message to some

Hula at Night, Etta As The Beast. Photo by Daniel Nicoletta

poor drag in a pink hoop skirt. With the house queen screaming as she evicted Pérez, the entire scene was awash in histrionics.

As they disappeared down the hall, I ran and pounded on Etta's door with her telegram in hand. "Etta …! Etta …!" But to no avail. I saw sister Ann in the hall and told her what had happened and how great She Fish looked dressed as a broken window. Ann sniggered, "Pérez would do anything to suck dick. Wouldn't we all? Ann started pounding on Etta's door, pleading and begging. "Telegram, Etta! Etta, telegram …!"

Pola sauntered by and asked if Etta was actually in the room. He tried to see through the keyhole but Etta had blocked it with her pink panties. We all wanted to know what she was doing with that Mandingo. Reluctantly, I started to slip the telegram under the closed door but Ann screamed, "STOP! Let's read it first."

We ripped open the envelope and devoured the contents. It seemed that Etta's family was going to have a surprise layover at the San Francisco Airport and they wanted Leslie to have breakfast with them in the morning. STOP. Fat chance of that. They may never see their gender fuck daughter again. We pounded on the door. "It's a telegram from your Dad, Linda"!

"Fuck it, Ann", I said as I slipped it under the door, frustrated at how much I wanted to see what was going on in there. I invited Ann back to my room to smoke. Pola disappeared. She does that.

"He never actually does anything here. Pola says she is an MGM romantic looking for Mr. Right. But she just walks around and watches us."

"We've got to watch out for her, girl," I responded. "She's known for his mouth, you know. Someday this is going to come back and haunt us"

"Who would believe her anyway?" Ann replied as Pola burst into the room.

"Are you two dishing me?" Pola demanded.

Oh God, we were caught in the act. And yet I noticed that after being at the baths for hours, not a hair on her head had been disturbed.

"Yeah girl, we were talking about you. Don't you know all the queens in town talk about you."

"Who talks about me?"

"You know who they are and probably who they've done as well."

"Well, yes, I probably do."

"And why don't you then tell us girls from the Hula Palace all there is to know?"

"No. I don't usually talk about anybody. Why? Who do you want to know about?"

"Drag Queens, SheMales, Trannies."

"Which Ones? The pretty ones or the ones running around with their hair on fire?"

"All of them, gurrll!"

"But there's so many and a lot of them hate me and each other. I must say, however, I have them all cataloged. First, I have the small 'p' professional drags that are so wrapped up in being pretty that they just don't have time for anyone else but themselves, especially if that someone doesn't serve their purposes. They are the queens who come to public functions after being in front of a mirror for hours, so full of makeup that they're extra ugly. This is the group that thinks they are to be adored anywhere they go. Unfortunately, it's usually only in the Tenderloin. The Tenderloin has better things to do than put up with their crap at Aunty Charlies.

"Then we have the fun professional drags that are pretty because it starts inside. They just put their make-up on to be extra pretty and hit the city streets. That's like Dale Evans and Nancy and most of that upper-crusty SIR group. The other half of that group falls in the professional ugly category. Those are real serious queens that fall apart after a few drinks and go home with the local new hustler in town who usually has more problems than just dealing with the drag. Those are the marriages made in hell, especially if the hustler eventually moves in. Status symbols, you know. Then it's George and Martha forever!"

Kreemah Ritz as Bette Davis as Jaws.
Photo by Ken Dickmann

"Next, of course, you also have real professionals who entertain like Lori Shannon. She's a good old girl. Charles Pierce falls into that too, though he never does drag offstage. Of course, we know he's a 'male actress.' Then sweetheart Roxy who hosted the Bette Davis Bus's on Halloween."

"Finally, you have the real women of the Tenderloin or those that wish they were real women but don't have the balls to really carry it off—or is that, cut it off? Most pathetic! Say, are you sure you want all this? It gets so complicated because you end up dealing with multiple personalities, and that's in any one person!"

She continues on, of course. I whispered to Ann, she can't believe all of this can she?

"Personally, my fave raves go to Michelle, Mavis, or Empress José who always have to remind these really serious queens that life is not to be taken so seriously. They hate Michelle and especially José for that. Of course, the gender fuck queens from the Cockettes like Pristine Condition, John Rothermel, Goldie Glitters, and Hibiscus—or like you two Hula Girls—are just too much for any of these queenly groups. Although of course Mavis, Michelle, José, Lori, Nancy and Dale and a few other exceptions just love you crazy girls."

"Then you try to get someone like a Pat Monclair on a Bette Davis Halloween bus dressed as Baby Jane and it would be next to impossible. No imagination. She belongs to the straight-glamour-queen syndrome that spends fortunes on costumes and rhinestone accessories just to walk around thinking she looks pretty. I mean, how many insincere compliments can one deal with in a night? But those queens believe every one of them! I prefer the tailored, Kay Francis look myself. I can be very grand with that look, but my hand is always free to hold a man where it's most important and where he prefers anyway."

With that a man caught Pola's eye, one that appeared to be exactly what her MGM sensibility required in the star department.

"Listen, girls, I think I gotta go. There's love walking around here unescorted. Drag queens—some good, some bad, some just plain folk. However, far be it from me to dish any of them. I know I'm pretty when I want to be, and when I'm not, I still get my cigarette lit. Ta, ta!" And with that Pola twirled out of the room just as we heard the MGM lion roar approval for her potential prey.

Didn't I tell you she was known for her mouth? Did I get a word in during her monologue? You should hear her on the phone. That's why we call her "Chatty Cathy."

Who the hell is Pat Monclair?

"Let me take this silly drag off and let's go look for a man." I changed into something dark and alluring, I'd stashed away in my bag. Where are my heels?

We went down the hall to stroll the stand-up orgy room. The second floor had the best erotic murals. I was hoping the door to the Flame Room was open. This hunky Latin number would always position his bed into the corner and lay on his tummy. It would look like the flames were coming out of his luscious melon ass. It was open and there he was. I called Ann over. What a vision. I wish I had my castanets. I stopped to admire his dark lanky body.

Ann grabbed my arm, dragging me away from the door. She wanted to smoke some more. She liked those tall and blonde numbers anyway. We did the bathhouse fast-walk down to the orgy room where we spun to find Brown Hanky Peter cruising the dark end. We sauntered over to offer him the joint and started chattering when he rudely told us to "Beat It." He was cruising the dude on the other side of the room. He told us it had taken him a half an hour to get this guy's attention. "So, beat it."

We looked across the room, then at each other, and giggled. We decided not to say a word. He had been looking in a mirror for the last whoever-knows-how-long.

We pressed on down the stairs for more coffee and drugs. This would make everything seem right. I wondered if Shirley was still tied up, where we had left her.

"Ann, we better check in on Shirley."

"Oh, she'll be fine." Ann was the perfect sister. We could dish anything with each other and because of our intoxicating habits we both had the assurance that neither one of us could remember a complete sentence by the morning. Life was grand!

As we landed on the lobby floor we saw Bunny behind the snack bar.

"What are you doing back there, Bunny?"

"I'm filling in for Rusty. He's late for his shift or maybe just tied up."

"No, I saw him on the third floor passing out Crisco on a silver tray like greasy hors d'oeuvres or whores d'oeuvres, if you will!

"Oh! Well, that's Rusty, always the host."

"Did you see She Fish?"

"Yeah, that Girl! Sadly, Glenda had to throw her out."

"How's Etta doing?"

"She's engrossed. She wouldn't open the door."

"I knew she would love this place. Her family is going to be in town tomorrow morning. He'll probably want me to go with her to the airport. I'll wear the Nancy Sinatra wig, which will stir it up a bit. HA!"

"Why doesn't she get out more?"

"She doesn't like to be alone on the streets and her knees hurt. You know all the gangs and bangs."

That's when Bunny started telling the story about how he had dressed as Ann Margaret for Halloween in one of my red leotards and my platinum wig which I never got back. We were chased by a gang of young white thugs who were out looking for sissies. We were on our way to a street festival on Polk Strasse for a Halloween Contest circa 1975. They challenged us on Folsom Street walking toward The Bolt.

They called Bunny a fag. She let them get closer and closer and then she showed the cute little buggers her lovely bat. Obviously, they'd had no idea that Bunny was prepared with a baseball bat under her gown or maybe one that was hidden in her soft spot. She ran after them like a wild woman in my good pumps screaming, "I'll bust your little virgin buts with this bat. You're going to ass bleed, you Fuckers!" She was convinced they wanted to kill us.

"If they really wanted to kill us all they would have to do is drop a little vile of germs at the baths and that would be that," Ann said.

"Nobody would do that," I countered.

"Don't be so sure," Ann said, "remember those black men in Alabama the government let sit around and die of syphilis so they could study their suffering but never told them. The government doesn't give a shit."

Anyway, right now we were laughing hysterically, thinking of that Halloween night with Bunny in that red leotard. I remember the moment vividly because of course I was right there with her, dressed as Nancy Sinatra, having trouble keeping up with my big sister in heels. Those kids ran like hell. It was so funny.

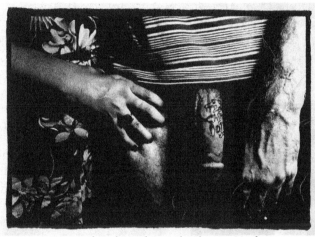

Boy Friend, Gurl Friend, Barracks, Photo Lee Mentley

"What's so funny, Princess?" It was Pola, resurfacing again and wondering what all the laughter was about.

"Her wig was funny, Pola. Bunny's wig—or was that my wig? Anyway, what happened to Mr. MGM, Pola?"

"He turned out to be too Warner Bros. Too serious, too heavy, and just too dull and boring. I've always hated most black-and-white films, anyway."

Pola had obviously been rejected and was trying to save face.

"I don't know, kids, how many more times I can walk about this place. I'm getting varicose veins going up and down these stairs. Mr. Right just doesn't exist, or at least not here. And I don't know if I'm ready for just lust. I've had that so many times but I don't think I can be tied up again and again hoping it will be "Him." I keep looking and looking, and then I give up and stop looking, and still nothing. I guess I'm looking for a meaningful relationship in all the wrong places, but I'm just not a cocktail-crowd person. I guess if I want MGM

I should take up singing lessons."

"Pola, we were just in the middle of a story about a wig."

"Oh, I'm sorry. I am depressed," she said, taking offense at our insensitivity to Pouting Pola's shattered dreams. "Laugh if you must, I don't care," retorted our rejected queen. "I'll play the game."

With that, just like Kay Francis, she lifted her head, and with that determined look exited the room to climb those well-worn, greasy stairs one more time in order to get laid by the first available man. We knew the men in the halls had no chance when Pola got that way. Half of her reputation was based on using sex as a weapon, even though she usually stabbed herself. The other half of her reputation was that he was seen with and dated the most gorgeous men in town. Entrances were one of her specialties. So were exits. Such a drama queen!

I was just going to ask Bunny if she still had that wig when he, the man of my dreams, walked in the door: Mr. Rocket.

I fluttered. The gurls froze up. No one took a breath such relationship moments are so fragile. Once Mr. Rocket won a free trip to Hawai'i just by running down to the Post Street Baths the night they had a "Bigger Than Yours" contest, joyfully displaying a dick that measured 16 and 1/2 inches. That's right honey! Right now, I was never so scared. He made me so nervous. I could savor this experience or it could be quick and hot. So many itchy possibilities for some nasty magic in the bath house hay. What would it be...? Oh God! This kind of lover is when twitter goes to twitch and your eyes spin.

Our eyes met. He knew what I wanted. He went into the lockers. I kissed Ann and Bunny good night. They said "Go get it, Gurlll." I decided I would run up the stairs and put my peignoir back on. Mr. Rocket loved to see me this way: hats, heels, miniskirts, big cars and lots of nerve.

"This will be a good night after all, GURRRLLLLSS!" I sashayed toward the steps, looking back over my sultry shoulder. I mentioned to the ladies, "Etta is not the only Princess to have her fantasy come true tonight." Up the stairs I went, for a moment thinking about Poor Pola.

Now ... where did I put that rubber butcher knife ...?

Painting and Photograph by Jim Campbell

EARTH MOTHER

Men

Something to trigger my anger
No man to pat my back
I reach for my pen
Hoping it could be more
Than my fist through the wall
Or a dead pet.
Where is he now
This over blown man of mine
Where is this fruitless fruit?

"Once a government is committed to the principle of silencing the voice of opposition, it has only one way to go, and that is down the path of increasingly repressive measures, until it becomes a source of terror to all its citizens and creates a country where everyone lives in fear." —Harry S. Truman

haiku on 330 grove

by ruth weiss

surrounded by white light

this structure housed deep with pride

and prophecy will

Let's call her "The Co-Chair." She was small, with butched-back hair, and he was a crusader for women's rights—or so she/he thought. Remember we are talking composite here, as I said in the introduction. Along with the word allegedly.

She wandered into my office in the Pride Foundation's Top Floor Gallery at 330 Grove Street one sunny San Francisco day. I sat back and said hello. I was browsing through a copy of Hustler. I had nominated the pig lawyer Walter Caplan aka The Wart for Hustler's "Asshole of the Month" column. Astonishingly, he hadn't been selected. I guess there might be bigger assholes than Wart out there, but it's hard to believe! Eventually he would be arrested and convicted for criminal offenses involving theft, fraud and as the judge said, moral turpitude.

Anyway, The Co-Chair was radiant, filled with the hope and glory of the new coming world. Her enthusiasm, however, outweighed his rhetoric.

Of course, I support women's rights, equal pay for equal work, and the privacy for women and men to control their own bodies. What I do not support is political aggression from men or women who proclaim they are feminist when actually they are fascist. Especially a small group of "Politically Correct" men and women that I will refer to as "Lizards," basically they are the same kind of people who surround Feinstein but would deny it. Later their heads would be all up her dress for a last chance at power.

The Lizard's idea of liberation operates from a dominant position of power, basically eating up whatever moves. That's because they think that power itself is the achievement. They do not realize that this is the trap the powerful have been stuck in forever. The Lizards turned the sexual revolution from a freedom to express oneself sexually into an opportunity to pursue the lust for profit and power.

Sometimes, they caused me to ask myself if my sexual liberation was really just lust for power? Is this why I wore a dress all these years—for power, not for fun? They are just plain wrong. The sexual revolution is about freedom outside moralistic constrictions, whether it was the right or the left wing's "Politically Correct" thinking. We need to respect each other's sexual and gender expressions and language, not acquire power over each other to continue communal slavery in yet another socially acceptable politically correct form. Just be a liberated person, period.

We are all different, and that is what makes us the same. We were fighting to challenge ancient religious and political assumptions that we should all think and act alike, and that there is no limit to differentiation. God forbid we should express ourselves without permission. Why was this so hard to figure out? For some, it was. All I could say is take off your clothes.

Initially, I kept these thoughts to myself. I had learned early on that these particular groups of Lizards were willing to be extremely abusive if you did not support their limited view of the universe. I have seen way to many politically correct feminists and their minions drunk on antiquated white male power.

As The Co-Chairs blathered on, I turned inward to reflect as I listened to their plans for the feminist agenda, one which ultimately would topple the male oligarchy, which was dominating the world, and replace everything with severe government and corporate grant whores on steroids. They somehow forgot that in the old world oligarchy there were already lots of women in power, women like DieAnne Feinstein, Phyllis Shafley and Anita Bryant. They may have been many things, but they were definitely not men and still fascists. An Unholy Trinity.

She told me that I wasn't supposed to be reading Hustler; it wasn't "Politically Correct." By the end of her diatribe on pornography, sex shops and my current pop hero Larry Flint, they invited me to participate in the blessing of a float—The Earth Mother—that had been created for "Take Back the Night" a feminist march on Broadway in North Beach. This is regular event among the "Politically Correct" who fear that pornography causes rape.

The Women's community has a well-founded, deep-seated fear of rape for obvious reasons. In our repressed, male-dominated society the entitled patriarchs were insatiable, sexist bastards. This comes from a time when Traditional Society rewarded men with women as trophies, like cattle sometimes they even called them "chattel." This worldview represents a deep-seated psychological disorder affecting those men who have not evolved along with the rest of society.

Most men are still raised today to be warriors, hunters, competitors and oppressors, whether it is on the battlefield or in the corporate board room. These are the main issues to be addressed—not dirty pictures or nude studies—and especially not in an art gallery where artists don't give a shit what sex you are or how you get off.

The kind of political march The Co-Chair was discussing, however, offered women's communities a worthwhile opportunity to discuss the issues, vent their accumulated righteous anger at male-oriented erotica, and create visibility in the media that they hope will educate the public to the women's agenda. That goal makes a lot of sense, politically.

On the other hand, I just do not believe pornography causes rape. Sick men are responsible for rape. Sick men who feel powerless commit rape for male approval. Sick, powerful men who cannot handle who they have become rape for self-esteem or for approval of other sick powerful men. Sometimes this same kind of rape is committed by women. Rape is a sickness. It's a criminal act. But, it's not an erotic expression derived from pornography. Most men never rape anybody—especially homosexual men—but according to The Co-Chair's way of thinking, only a dead man never commits rape.

In any case, a variety of political organizations are ready to go to gaudy North Beach on a moment's notice and chant "Two, four, six, eight—why don't you all just masturbate?" I marched with them once, out of a perverse sense of political obligation. I understood their motivation, not their target. I had personally been the victim of a sexual assault at an early age by other kids. I have also been beaten, knifed, pistol whipped, hit in the skull with a chain, and hunted down and shot at before I was the age of 16 because of my sexual orientation, wild style of dress, and my all too obvious hairy/feminine qualities.

My wearing big flowered print Hawaiian mu'u mu'us in high school was a classic no-no; I was too visibly girlish to live safely in an East Los Angeles ghetto.

Broken Dishes Flyer. Photo by David Greene

Unfortunately, for better or worse, I understand the fear and the pain of assault on a very personal level directly, so I brought my hairy tits up to Broadway the last time they marched, just to make my political sisters happy.

I remember chanting "Shut it down! Shut it down!" in front of the Mabuhay Gardens where artist friends Dolores De-Luce formerly Dolores Deluxe and Amber Waves were performing their hilarious original production of Broken Dishes, a story of true confessions and beauty secrets from Allusions to Prime Time, a camp on the life of Wacky Wacs and the Hello Wheeze Show, with music composed and performed by Cockette composer Scrumbly Koldewyn and lyrics by Martin Worman aka Philthee Ritz. Dolores and Amber belted such memorable tunes as "The Vulcan Vamp," "The Burning Bush," "The Hot Tub Blues," " It's A Scream" and "The Rhinestone Blues." I kept hoping

Lee Mentley speaking at The Robert Hillsborough Memorial in Golden Gate Park, June 24, 1978. Harvey Milk (circled) in attendance. Photo by Daniel Nicoletta

that Dolores would come out the front doors and spot me chanting. After all, it was Dolores and Amber who were actuaaly liberated. We could have had a real good roar together.

I looked up from my musings. The Co-Chair was still here in my office. I thought to myself as he ranted, "How much longer can she go on?"

Somehow, these frightful groups of neo-leftist, non-revolutionaries are supposed to be on the cutting edge of change. I think they are actually just more of the same old political bullshit wrapped in a new package. They involve themselves in all sorts of nasty shenanigans and fight over who is the most "Politically Correct." These Lizard Queens were out to control the women's community, the lesbian community, and the so-called gay male community. For God's sake, who wants to model a new world based on these tired old power-driven patterns?

The new power brokers were very abusive to anyone they considered not "Politically Correct." One of the female volunteers at 330 Grove allegedly had had her tires slashed by one of their ilk. She wasn't submissive enough and would not spy on the Pride Foundation for them. I felt so sorry for her. She was a single mother and really couldn't afford this kind of harassment. Of course, we could never prove who had done it, but we had a good idea. One way or another, we would all have to pay for the intellectual pluralism we were nurturing at the Pride Center.

I looked up again. The Co-Chair was still standing there. Honestly, would she never leave? This is not the kind of drag performance I enjoy.

I went back once again to my own thoughts, remembering an afternoon a while ago when Ms. Twiddle E Dee, a woman who would frighten any lumberjack up a tree, came into the gallery to complain about gay male art. She had singled out an incredibly beautiful painting of Joe Dellasandro as David, painted by Demetrie Kabbaz in honor of Michelangelo's birthday.

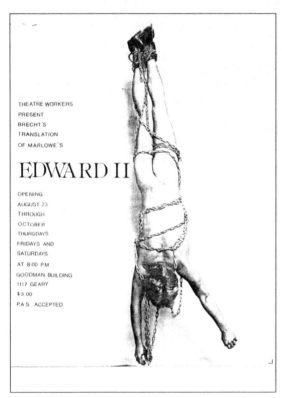

THEATRE WORKERS
PRESENT
BRECHT'S
TRANSLATION
OF MARLOWE'S

EDWARD II

OPENING
AUGUST 23
THROUGH
OCTOBER
THURSDAYS
FRIDAYS AND
SATURDAYS
AT 8:00 P.M
GOODMAN BUILDING
1117 GEARY
$3.00
P.A.S. ACCEPTED

King Edward Flyer. Artist unknown

The painting was a seven-foot-tall representation shaped like a stained glass window from a modern cathedral. It pictured a reclining nude Dellasandro in full proud display of his famous male genitalia, a part of him that Andy Warhol had made immortal in the underground film Trash in which Dellasandro had starred with New York celebrity Holly Woodlawn.

Demetrie's David had previously been censored by the San Francisco Police Department at the 1975 Art Expo held throughout the week prior to the Castro Street Fair. When we put together the second street fair, we requested that the Castro Village Association merchants donate their store windows to display new art created in the community. When The David was spotted by the SFPD they wanted it removed, eventually making us put a black banner across its luscious cock. We added the words "Censored by the SFPD" on the shroud over David's manhood. Demetrie was so excited to show the Dellasandro at the Top Floor Gallery because he thought; at last, he wouldn't be censored.

This obvious psychological threat from Ms. Twiddle Dee really pushed all my buttons. Her group hated men, thinking it was open season on dick. This fucking fascist bitch had no respect for dick art, I thought, but she wants to use our gallery for a rap session. I said to myself, "Fuck that!" Twiddle Dee had been offered the gallery to host her event but now she wanted certain paintings removed because they would remind her of being with men or raped. Essentially, if she could have, she would have trashed anything in the gallery that didn't meet her standards of "Politically Correct."

I bellowed "Ann, get out here and listen to this shit." I turned and saw Ann, aka Jimmy Coker, coming. I looked at Ms. Dee and said "You fucking never stop and think how many of us men have been beaten to death because we love dick." I told her that we weren't working here in this gallery, or in this center, or in this movement, in order to put the cock back into the closet for anybody. If she didn't like it she could stay the fuck out of the gallery or just go where she felt more comfortable and safe—someplace where there were no dicks.

I went on an emotional rant and forcefully explained that the cock on Joe Dellasandro, or on Michelangelo's or Demeitre Kabbaz's David, was not interested in raping her tired old ass or any of the women coming to her event. I told her "the male body is sacred to other men, just like the female body is sacred to you." The painting would stay.

She persisted in threatening the art. I explained to her that her support of the Equal Rights Amendment gave me the opportunity to handle her the same way I would any other person who might attack art: I would punch her fucking lights out and hang her on the wall if she attempted to destroy any art in this gallery.

Ann moved in front of The David. I knew I was capable of downing this galoot if I had to and Demetrie would absolutely kill me if I let this obsessed, man-hating fascist ruin his masterpiece. I insisted she leave the gallery at once. She resisted at first but realized my resolve. She departed in a thunderous stomp. "Get the fuck out of here! Can you believe this shit? Who are these fucking idiots?" I raged.

"Sit, Princess!" Ann said. I did. My breath had been taken away but Ann did her best to calm my nerves. I had been raised by six Italian Gypsy women, so I had never felt this kind of anger toward women before. At least I knew it was just this small group of hateful Lizards and not the prevailing attitude in the Lesbian Community. Even so, Ann would not give up. She always felt I was too radical and had to be moderated, so she insisted a compromise be on the agenda.

At Ann's request, we placed a four-paneled folding screen painted in washed oils of the Marquees of Market Street by Jim Campbell in front of the censored-once-again male icon. They still had the nerve to complain, but the Lizards certainly didn't have the political savvy of their newly found mentor Supervisor Milk. The screen would have to do. I couldn't believe the closed-minded greed of this self-loathing, megalomaniacal fool, so wrapped up in her own political fortunes that the rest of humanity becomes irrelevant.

Once again, I've never had anything but respect for the women's community, but I never felt we had to share everything we did in the Pride Center with them either. These particular lesbians, however, needed to learn to respect gay men and not blame our gender as a whole for their own miserable life experiences. I really wished they would keep their pushy acts in some other center—maybe one for the Politically Angry?—and just stay out of the Pride Center entirely. Across town this same cadre enjoyed a Women's Center. Men were not allowed in the door until some show down changed the equation.

Men needed a private place where they could be vulnerable and open up to other men, but the Lizards would say "That's Not Politically Correct." The men that had been gathering in the safety of the Pride Center had problems they needed to work out with other men. We had as much to fear from the so-called "Moral Majority" as they did. Yet these controlling Lizards saw us as people who needed a course correction and be retrained into their "Politically Correct" Co-Chairperson world. They were literalists, impervious to meaning, because they were unable to recognize our personal rights of experience to have a vibrant and full life as men, and not be the fossil-like primates they imagine us to be. Some of their boy Lizards loved the training and validated their inroads into the men's community.

The male and female artists of the Top Floor Gallery did not, however! We demanded our own space in which to discover our artistic selves. How much clearer could it be? Downstairs was the Pride Center, a gay center, where they could have their fucking meetings as far as I was concerned. The Top Floor Gallery was not the place for it.

I left the building and went to the Baths. Since they had successfully turned our exciting center into a sexist battlefield, I needed to "prey."

The Lizards with their misplaced resentment towards men, along with their so-called nouveau-glitter-chic, fell into the very traditional greed trap. They were joined there by the innocent and naive who believed everything they read in the gay rags, eventually giving everything we had created away. Even in the 1980s in LA with the Hillside Murders where gay men were being murdered and decapitated, they tried to keep it all quiet since it was happening near gay bars. They didn't want us to go public with that kind of story. They were little more than death merchants.

In the same way, the whole thriving community center was eventually handed over to the Corporatists in the Democratic Party alongside the new Gay Machine. It was just as Spider Queen Feinstein wanted things. She knew how to work these political neophytes. She always came out on top, and the Fags who were coyly ensconced in their gay ghetto bought what she was offering hook, line, and sinker.

The whole situation left such a bad taste in my mouth that I went out and registered Republican—Not really! I vote Green. All of this happened before the shit hit the proverbial fan.

Back to the present — Unbelievably, The Co-Chair is still ranting away in my office. I respectfully declined her offer of joining the blessing of the float saying "I have a prior engagement. Maybe next year." Somehow she believed me, leaving my office with an assured confidence she had converted me into her newest clone in the Neo-Matriarch movement. I sat back with a little smirk on my face, glanced over at Ann, he smirked too.

Paul Hardman was President of the Pride Foundation, a community-based legal organization dedicated to litigation and legislative lobbying concerning equal human rights for sexual minorities. Paul Hardman had accused The Gay Freedom Day Parade Committee of alleged fiscal irresponsibility. It was about to become a sticky issue. A Flock of Lizards controlled the embattled committee.

The Lizards were obsessed in owning and controlling, or destroying anything created through a democratic process that did not worship at the feet of their delusions of Gaydom changed into the GLBTQURSTUV Community. Divided we fail, we are Gay. The Co-Chairs, The Wart, and other specific Lizardlings would be subpoenaed before the week was out for refusing to provide Pride Foundation with important financial documents related to a rather clumsy attempt to own The Gay Freedom Day Parade, The Gay Community Center, and, I guess, anything that had the word Gay. I was getting really sick of the word "Gay," There was nothing gay about this kinda shit! I didn't feel Gay just Pissed Off!

Wildly respected Gay Rights Advocates attorney Matthew Coles represented the parade committee, with help from the lawyer Walter Caplan aka Wart. I suspected they were two more of the new "Gay Machine's Kingpins" or better yet, "Queenpins!. I couldn't stand Walter Caplan, who was eventually reported in the San Francisco papers in 1989 as the man who attempted to have the Gay AIDS Vigil participants thrown in jail for camping out in front of the federal building and disturbing his cafe patrons at United Nations Plaza. On the other hand, Matthew Coles was a reasonable chap but I felt he was misguided, yet not as much as the other prominent Gay Lizards, who had their faces so far up Supervisor Feinstein's ass they could smell brunch.

It seemed that the Pride Foundation had stepped on Democratic Party territory. Supervisor Feinstein wanted us out of our building at 330 Grove so she could park her car and walk to the opera without seeing poor people. She wanted Paul Hardman out of her filthy dirty, starched hair.

Conservative Supervisor Quintin Kopp had informed Paul Hardman that a group of unnamed individuals had attempted to swap title pages on the Pride Foundation's Gay Community Center grant application. Of course this was a move by the Lizards to own the community center and ensure power over the community. There were also allegations that the Tavern Guild was accused of hoarding tens of thousands of dollars they had collected that was earmarked for the Gay Community Center. Paul made the Lizardling grant junkies at City Hall upset when he uncovered their little charade. Paul knew their names and he reminded them that stealing federal dollars is a felony.

The Tavern Guild was chagrined because the Pride Foundation had an alcoholic recovery program. The Tavern Guild didn't want anyone to know that at that time 85% of their clients were suffering from alcoholism. No one wanted to hear that ugly truth. They only wanted money and power and as long as things looked good in the press, they were happy.

Paul Hardman was adamant about protecting the Pride Foundation's tax-exempt status and demanded an audit of the Parade Committee's financial records. He accused them of gross mismanagement and fraud for tampering with the Pride Foundation's proposal. He insisted on accounting for the dough they had collected in Pride's name.

While all of this was brewing, I had been in Hawai'i all summer creating Isolation Enterprises and Time Release Records with elegant yet severe Helen, a drug dealer who patronized the arts, our own gay Daddy Warbucks. We had

Painting by William McNeil. Chairs and small painting by Curator. First National Lesbian Art Show, Nikki Schrager. The Top Floor Gallery, 330 Grove, SF, CA, circa 1978. Photo by Daniel Nicoletta

successfully signed the New Wave musical acts of Tuxedomoon, Winston Tong and Los Microwaves, we spent two months in a remote plantation house in cozy Puwela Valley on Maui with horses, lots of wild chickens and plenty

74

Gay Freedom Parade in protest of Anita Bryant. From left to right, Jimmy Coker, Pérez, Lee Mentley, Pamela Goodlow and Glen Stroud. Photographer Unknown

aloha spirit. I love being in Hawai'i. The Polynesian culture is so rich; they have so much to offer our struggling planet. Anyway, I was fortunate to have missed most of the arguing and shouting, but I returned full of aloha and just in time for the opening night of our First National Lesbian Art Show, put together by the artistic talents of Nikki Schrager in the Top Floor Gallery.

What I walked into was a real horror. Paul and The Co-Chair had a real blowout at the opening of the art show that shocked me. I had liked The Co-Chair at first when I left for the Islands. All was well. We had had a very successful parade and the committee should have been able to close-up shop and by next year have their own 501(c)(3). Then, Ann clued me in about how the financial records books had disappeared overnight. I even found checks made out to the Parade Committee in the trash the next day. They were so sloppy about it all. Bottom line: it was impossible to believe these people had the best interest of the community in mind.

It reminded me something that happened at the 1977 Gay Freedom Day Parade. As I was walking up the steps to the stage to speak to the gay crowd, I saw the editor of the San Francisco Sentinel Charles Morris and a well-known politician plus a few volunteers dragging a huge pile of money on a large tarp into the Convention Center from the main stage. The crowd had been whipped into excitement by the anti-Anita Bryant speech delivered by State Assemblyman Willie

Brown. It was so exciting to be a part of the 1977 march. The crowd was wild with joy because we had finally arrived on the world stage. Thank you, Anita Bryant! The crowd just passed their generous donations forward to the stage; the loot was dumped onto the tarp and off it went, never to be seen again.

I didn't think about the money again until the following year when we still had $12,000 in unpaid bills and no one seemed to know where that pile of money had gone. Chuck Morris said it was used to pay other bills, but there was no record

Pride Foundation at 330 Grove. Photo by Pérez

to back this up, nor of how much money had been collected. This made funding agencies uneasy about giving money to a committee with no legal standing.

The next year, the 1978 Parade Committee approached the Pride Foundation and asked for help. The city wouldn't release funds the Supervisors had appropriated for the 1978 parade until The Gay Freedom Day Committee had a 501(c)(3) tax exempt organization to safeguard the donations. The Pride Foundation had the credibility that funding sources wanted to see. The board agreed and attached the Gay Freedom Day Parade to the Pride Foundation as an independent standing committee.

Pride volunteers cleaned and painted offices, and provided desks, a private bathroom, phones, office supplies, and file cabinets. However, the Lizards on the committee didn't like Paul Hardman's conservative nature and the by-the-book legal philosophy of The Pride Board. They were always plotting against Paul. I never understood the adversity towards the Pride board of directors since the only demand was for an accounting after the parade. Soon enough, they would have their own 501(c)(3). Nonetheless, they never wanted to acknowledge what Pride had done for the community, legally and socially. I suspect it was because we were not "Politically Correct," neither were we Co-Chairperson-types nor emasculated men or so I thought.

You would think that after Harvey Milk's HOPE Speech downstairs on how this building had a soul and was so vital to the movement they would have respect for what we were building?

When the parade was over and it was time for accountability, it was undeniable that the parade committee had made the books disappear. What a mess! I hated politics, especially these neo-glitter fags that became fashionable on the fear campaigns generated by Anita Bryant. They wanted money and power and had no idea what it was to be gay. They were only interested in their own personal political agendas that had nothing to do with liberation. As much as the Ku Klux Klan hates Queers and Catholics, they despised those of us in the gay community who had created the street movements of the seventies without salaries and grants. In some ways, with this kind of greedy professional rising up from the muck, this was no longer our movement. I wanted to throw up.

"Ann, why am I always throwing people out of places? I must have been a severe landlord in a prior life." We giggled like schoolgirls. I tried to change focus as I glanced out the curved Spanish brick windows built from the wharf ruins of the 1906 earthquake. Maybe we too could rise again from the ashes.

I loved the natural colorations of ancient brick in this building, the mold, the moss, and the ivy covered air wells. It reminded me of a special tree that was covered with romantic ivy near my childhood home and the man I was in love with in college. He had surprised me with a first kiss one night on LSD while watching 2001: A Space Odyssey at the Grand Pantages Theatre in Hollywood. Afterwards we went to the Los Angeles Civic Center to swim in the colorfully lit fountains and waterfalls below the Music Center. We poured dish soap into the jets and splashed through the prismatic bubbles and giant suds till we were slick and soft. We made hot, passionate love all night. I wished he was with me now, my knight in white satin.

Back to the Top Floor Gallery ...

There were seven extremely large peaked sky lights gracing the 22 foot high oak beamed ceilings. The sun streamed in like a silver blaze on the Sequoia colored red brick of what was originally The Bear Photography Building. Fifty thousand square feet of open industrial space on three floors with a horseshoe shaped mezzanine.

I thought about the history of this great building. Years before, Paul Hardman had convinced newly elected Mayor Moscone to let us use the building as a Gay Community Center meeting place. In return, the Mayor wanted us to help deal with the increasing problem of runaways forced into hustling on Polk Street in order to survive.

Paul helped many of the young street people, even bailing some of them out of jail. These great kids had been abandoned by their intolerant families. Once they heard our doors were open—in fact, they were left unlocked—they came in off the streets in droves so they could sleep unmolested. They called themselves The Pride and chose the lion as their symbol.

With their eager help we rapidly and secretly renovated on the first floor of the formerly condemned structure into a vibrant, functioning resource center for their needs— but no one could know we allowed them to sleep there! These were good kids and we wanted to give them a chance to contact their parents and try to re-unite them with their families, much in the same way we had at The Hula Palace.

Over and over again, I heard families with the nerve to say they were good Christians yet didn't want their troubled kids back. They have no idea what it really means to believe The Christ. I pity American families who have thus far failed their homosexual children, leaving them to be used by the scum who pollute the world. I assume it is a sin against any God not to love your own children.

I may have often felt like Major Barbara, or dear Florence Nightingale, but Paul was the real hero. It was Paul who offered our organization, The Eureka/Noe Valley Artist Coalition, the third floor of 330 Grove St. as an artist gallery and studio space. We couldn't refuse. It was an artist's dream come true. The artists were given autonomy from Pride's Gay Center on the first two floors and a small amount of funding from the Neighborhood Arts Program. In return we helped paint the rest of the building and organized social activities for the foundation. We also answered the emergency phone lines at night, serving as live-in security while maintaining the suicide prevention hotline.

As we cleaned and shoveled through years of rubble, we discovered more and more about the building's unique history. The Cockettes once lived in the loft we now called the Top Floor Gallery. We also learned this had been the rehearsal space for many of the sixties greatest rock acts, including Janice Joplin and The Dead, probably because it was located just a few blocks from the infamous Fillmore. It had also been the scene of Allen Ginsberg's so-called first drag poetry reading, a tradition the Hula Palace carried on to honor the great howling sage.

Paul Hardman also found evidence in the basement he said showed the building had been used as a major staging area for radical political groups and rumored that included the Black Panthers. It had been the first Black Community Cultural Center funded under the San Francisco Arts Commission and home to a dance company surprisingly named the Black Light Explosion. They took up living on the second floor while presenting performances

330 Grove Flyer. Design by Adrian Craig

on the first floor. In the early 70s, it was also functioned as a rehearsal and living space for the magical theater group "The Angels of Light." No wonder the establishment hated this building!

Paul surmised it was where Patty Hearst had been kept for a while during her SLA kidnaping. He claimed to have found documents produced by the SLA in the basement which he turned over to the office of the Chief of Police. Paul loved to theorize, but who knows—anything was possible regarding this space.

Once again, I'm drawn to the present to notice that only now is Co-Chair finished wandering through the gallery and slowly descending the stairs.

How I wished they would just "get it"—why couldn't they learn to share?

But right now, what I needed was a deep breath. I moved like an arching lion, stretching back, then over, breathing in deeply, then raising up and exhaling. I opened my eyes. Yep, it was still the 1970s and I could see the grandeur of the Opera House out the Spanish windows against a bright blue sky, along with the stern dark dome of City Hall. How could anything filled with such architectural splendor, so majestic, be so spotted with blood? What a mystery power-seekers are. No wonder they say you can't fight City Hall. "Just breathe!" I kept telling myself.

The rest of the week was booked with what seemed like endless meetings, rehearsals, lawyers, and an evening with the enlightened Republican Senator Milton Marks' reelection committee. Then a good surprise happened.

I was asked to perform in Edward II at the Goodman Building. I got a call on Monday from Michael McKenna who told me a cast member had been in an accident and they needed me on stage Thursday. I would have no rehearsal with the cast. I would only have an hour with the director. Could I do this? My cousin Marla was arriving from Los Angeles to spend the weekend. Okay. Let's see. Brecht's translation of Marlowe's Edward II in four days. What should I do?

This would give me the opportunity to be on stage with David Baker Jr., whom I greatly admired and Billy Buttons whose buttons I adored. "Should I do it Ann?" She just smiled. "They want to know right now." She knew I couldn't say no. All that handsome flesh on stage, plus I needed a break from the bullshit in this building. "I love King Edward, I'll be right up," I told them, and turning to Ann, "I'm going to the Goodman Building!"

I ran down to Van Ness to jump the #47 bus. It was crowded so I had to stand. I had on tight-fitting black Frisco jeans. A hefty matron with hefty lips sitting on the seat below me couldn't stop looking at my crotch and was making me feel uneasy she really wasn't my type. Finally she looked up and said, "That sure does look healthy." I got off the bus. I couldn't help but be amazed at how some people love cock and some people want to cut them all off. What a mystery!

I walked the rest of the way. When I got to the Goodman Building I bumped into Thumper. It felt like a homecoming. It would be so great to be in this production. I grabbed the script and walked through my blocking with director Ken Wilkinson.

Afterwards, I went upstairs to visit Michelle Linfante who was working with an interesting new women's theater collective, Lilith. I wanted to invite them to perform at Top Floor Gallery. They eventually went off to Europe and performed at the 1979 Festival of Nations in Germany, then they toured California, the Pacific Northwest, and Canada where they won an award for a play entitled Moonlighting. Michelle was also very active in the fight to save the Goodman Building from the redevelopment agency who had taken the building from Mr. Goodman in questionable condemnation proceedings. This was very much like what was being attempted on Grove Street now.

October 20, 1978

san Francisco seen ──────── byseeGULL

HARVEY
MILK MILK
HOMOGENIZED
COMMUNITY
CENTER

"WHO says we never OUTGrow OUR Need FOR MILK?"

The artists tried buying the building but the agency sold out to developer Alan Wofsy. He claimed he would develop it along with the artists and assured everyone that they would be able to continue to live in their studios. Of course, Wofsy quickly betrayed them. Somehow he was able to retain special classifications and benefits the artists had received from redevelopment although he eventually destroyed all THEIR live-in work space and upgraded it to a gentrified enclave and curiosity shops. It seems dishonor was everywhere in this city.

Lamenting the seemingly hopeless politics of the preservationists in the face of the politically powerful, an alliance was formed between the tenants of the International Hotel in Chinatown and those of us at 330 Grove. We hoped if we could also get the support of The Victorian Alliance we would have a better chance of saving these wonderful buildings. We believed if we were recognized as being at risk from the same forces that threatened the Victorian architecture of San Francisco, we would be able to lend our support in saving the incredible City of Paris, The Victorian department store on Union Square.

Back to the Goodman ...

Michelle and I set up a meeting at the Top Floor Gallery to schedule a Lilith drama, and then I went off for a walk down Geary to Polk. I walked up to Pine Street and had dinner at the Grub Stake.

Thursday afternoon my cousin Ms. Marla, who was Ms. Patty Duke's secretary at the Screen Actors Guild on Sunset in Hollywood, arrived with Ms. Cody, whose grandfather was Buffalo Bill Cody. Who can figure how this all happens? After all, I'm just a drag queen from East LA!

I invited my family to the Goodman Building but I did not tell them I was actually in the play. I love surprises. When we arrived, I showed them to their seats. I excused myself, telling them I wanted to say hello to friends backstage. In the first scene, my character leans passionately against a stone wall upstage observing the King and his lover. Shortly after my entrance, draped in yellow fabric over my otherwise nude body, I was sniffing poppers as I heard cousin Marla heckle from the audience, "Fucking Leroy, what the fuck are you doing up there?"

The opening scene was a raucous one set at the baths and it covered the foul mouth of my dear adorable cousin. "This was why your family doesn't visit you," she kidded me later. We had a great laugh and a memorable San Francisco weekend. On Sunday, they returned to LA LA Land. She wrote me a thank you note and insisted that on her next vacation she wanted me to find her an available man, as handsome as my friends in the theater. Those sweet boys sure did look good and that is what it's all about—Ah, men!

Sunday evening my schedule brought me to an old Neighborhood Arts Program facility on Brannon Street. Of course, I wore black, since it was South of Market.

This was the night the subpoenas were going to be served to The Gay Freedom Day Parade Committee. I was to attend the meeting as a witness for the serving agent and say nothing, just observe.

What a sad joke! The Great Empress of San Francisco, José Sarria, had set us queens free to be who we were and these political faggots couldn't get it. They were trying to make us into neo-left wing clones like we were some sort of social silly nutty putty. We were supposed to respectfully fall into their political kick line so they could own houses up on Buena Vista and terrorize the fashionable by fucking in the park. Not the Lesbians, just the Queens were fucking in the bushes. I Think?

The meeting was orchestrated into oblivion where they say nothing, do nothing, and are nothing but a pain in the ass. Sitting in the back I excused myself quietly to the men's room for some fresh air.

Going down the stairs I noticed The Earth Mother, the float that had presumably graced Broadway's parade the night before. It was stationed by the back freight entrance. It looked wonderful and at this point in the evening a truly gay diversion from the gray meeting. I went to give it a look when Keith, a bureaucratic friend from downtown was coming in the front door. We embraced "kissy kissy" and he joined me in quiet conversation as we meandered over to The Earth Mother. He wanted to know more about the subpoenas. The dish was spreading. Good!

The float was large, maybe sixteen feet long and eight or ten wide, on a rented truck bed covered with endless real and paper flowers that created a beautiful illusion of the earth, her mountains, rivers, and fertile lands. At the top of the earth was a figure of a Goddess with lush hair and a crown of flowers on her head. As we walked around in front of the float, the imaginary waters of the bed swooped up to the hems and became the starred garment of the Earth Mother.

Having opened the garment covering the image of the Goddess, they were already taking the float apart. We could see the wooden-framed cross that led up to the head of the Earth Mother. That's when we saw it: a dead pig. A real, gutted-open, crucified fucking dead pig! "Oh my God, it's a dead fucking pig!" Its mouth was open, like it had been screaming.

Keith and I both leaned in, mouths open. We couldn't believe what we saw. Then we took a few steps back and with the quick flutter of our hands we fanned away the putrefied stench. We just looked at each other horrified and not knowing what to say. We left quickly, astonished and sickened at this bizarre discovery. We hurried up the stairs back to the parade meeting, each sitting alone with our thoughts.

Could the Lizards have done this? Was this the same float? What could it mean? Had someone actually tortured this poor animal? Who had done this? I didn't want to know!

I heard a commotion and looked up to see the subpoenas being served. "You want potatoes with that?" I wanted to say as I chuckled to myself. The Co-Chairs took the envelope and slipped it into a folder, not making any reference to the document. I suppose they did not want anyone to know they had been subpoenaed. I guess that makes perfect sense if you're stealing a movement on one floor and allegedly crucifying a pig on another.

But once again, I had to wonder, "Who the hell are you people...?"

Harvey Milk on Castro Street. Photo by Daniel Nicoletta

Lee Mentley at SF City Hall the day after the White Night Riots,
May 22, 1979. Photo by Daniel Nicoletta

THE KNIGHT WAS A PAWN

Brothers in Arms
Who goes so far into freedom
That he cannot see the illusion.
He moves through the streets
Separate from it all
Except fashion
Posture
It seems to make it all belong.

Two men lie dead. While standing in the moonlight, tens of thousands of citizens from the Bay Area bear candles and cellophane-covered flashlights. They descend upon San Francisco's City Hall to pay homage to two great public servants, the Honorable Mayor George Moscone and charismatic populist San Francisco Supervisor Harvey Milk. Among the tears and outburst of mourning, the city is asking, "How did this bloody deed happen?"

San Francisco politics had become a disjointed chess game.

85

* * *

Friday afternoon I had an appointment with San Francisco Supervisor Harvey Milk at City Hall, a short walk from my office in The Top Floor Gallery at the Pride Foundation's Gay Community Center, 330 Grove Street. I participated in all of Harvey's political campaigns. In some ways, he had become my New American Hero.

The normally brilliant cool San Francisco air hung with the distasteful sweet psychological smell of the Kool-Aid Deaths a week before. The Reverend Jim Jones had just killed all of his followers in Guyana. It was now the day after Thanksgiving and it seemed that San Francisco was coming unraveled with fear and grief.

Although, as Harvey advised, I never miss a chance to work the grand marble staircase of City Hall, today it's a walk through an echoless, near empty space. I stopped in the legislative offices and chatted with Anne Kronenberg, Harvey's top legislative aide. "Good to see you, Lee. Harvey is around somewhere," she said. Then she told me she was going to see her family Monday somewhere up in Oregon or Washington. It sounded like fun and she really needed a break from all the chaos. She was a solid rock for the community.

I walked across to the Supervisor's Chambers. Through an open door I could hear Harvey talking to his glitter-rock aide, Dick Pabich. I slipped into Harvey's small private chamber and waited for him. It reminded me of my high school counselor's office. It even smelled the same—asbestos, I suspect. I counted the holes in the ceiling until Pabich leaves, just like school again. With exceptions of Harvey's top two aides, Anne Kronenberg and Carl Carlson, I did not trust the politicos who surrounded Harvey since he had been elected. No one was sure what their agenda was, but money was in the political air more than ever before. I took a deep breath. Believe me, focused breathing would become very important this week.

Confronting Harvey was never easy. I loved this guy but he could be a jerk and it seemed to be happening more and more lately. We could only hope he wasn't selling out his supporters in the preservationist community. Breathe ...!

I was there to ask Harvey what was going on concerning my position as a Neighborhood Organizer for the San Francisco Art Commission's Neighborhood Arts Program. I was expecting to reconfirm his support for the 330 Grove Street Building and my position. This seemed reasonable since Harvey had given an amazing speech the night he declared his run for Supervisor. In his speech he praised 330 Grove, underscoring how important we were to the movement. He even remarked that the building had a soul. Now I needed to know if the rumors were true or not, if he was going to change his vote on the demolition of the famous City of Paris building on Union Square.

I definitely had reasons to be concerned. The President of the Victorian Alliance, Earl Moss, had called this morning. I was in my office at the Top Floor Gallery in the 330 Grove building. In a panic he had asked if Harvey was deserting the preservationist ship. He had heard from Pacific Heights matrons that Milk made a deal to vote against preserving the City of Paris. Earl also told me some dark news about dangerous, nasty rumors running the streets involving more deaths coming from the People's Temple Massacre. Later that same day Margo St. James, San Francisco's highest profile Madame, told me she had heard from her Working Girls at COYOTE 'Call Off Your Old Tired Ethics' that political figures including Harvey had been targeted for assassination.

My head was spinning. I tried to think of a lighter time. Like when JoAnn came running into the Hula Palace after watching Harvey get a blow job in the store front window at Tommy's Plants...! Ha...? Breath ...,

Not supporting the City of Paris preservation would be a dramatic turn-around in Harvey's position. I continued to hope he wasn't selling out his environmental support. The French had built and opened the City of Paris, notable for its magnificent Victorian rotunda that at Christmas time, to the city's great enjoyment, held the largest Christmas tree in this part of the world. At the top of the rotunda was an exquisite stained glass depiction of clipper ships that brought European merchandise to San Francisco before the Panama Canal was built. The fine artistry of stained glass honored the sailors who had risked their lives keeping San Francisco in touch with European civilization and commerce. In short, the City of Paris was the essence of old San Francisco. You could say it was the location of The City's heart equal only to the Victorian Garden Court at the Palace Hotel. If Harvey was going to vote for demolition, this would mean an end to our easygoing, longtime political relationship.

This is exactly why I didn't want to get involved with Harvey or San Francisco politics to begin with. Harvey had convinced me that he would be different and we could make the difference for our community. The Gay community would finally have a safe and honest place to live. And of course that thought scared the hell out of the Power Shakers who were now getting ready for the kill. San Francisco was becoming Wall Street West. In the financial games being played, perhaps suddenly it was time to call in the development chips.

I informed Earl Moss I had been conveniently dismissed from my position at the San Francisco Arts Commission's Neighborhood Arts Program. This was done under the guise of Proposition 13 but privately I was told by my Director that ironically the dismissal came because of the success I had at 330 Grove's Top Floor Gallery.

The Neighborhood Arts Program had been funding the Top Floor Gallery at 330 Grove. Our exhibits had attracted favorable notice in the art columns of the local press, especially the Seven from Black Mountain show with Paul Alexander, Ruth Asawa, Mary Bowles, Knute Styles, Etta Deikman, Tom Field, William McNeil, and with a reading by poet Robert Duncan. Soon after this show, we exhibited Black Mountain master painter Caldwell Brewer. Brewer was presented to us by local South of Market artist Allie Bill Skelton, with the show being produced by none other than Robert De Niro, Sr. who was himself a Black Mountain artist. This was the first time Mr. De Niro ever stepped out from the closet. Both of these exhibits helped focus attention on the drive to save 330 Grove from the wrecking ball.

TO EXPLAIN BLACK MOUNTAIN:

DERSTVRM: THE DEGENERATE ART OF GERMANY:

The art of the German Bauhaus led the way for 20th century modern art and expressionism. The German and French artists were viciously attacked and persecuted by the NAZI. Those that could, fled to the USA. There they created the Chicago Institute of Design and the Black Mountain School of the arts in Tennessee.

Renowned Black Mountain artists moved to the San Francisco Bay Area where some of them participated and exhibited at the Hula Palace Salon's Top Floor Gallery at 330 Grove Gay Pride Community Center 1977 & 1978. Artists such as Paul Alexander, Ruth Asawa, Mary Bowles, Knute Styles, Etta Deikman, Tom Field, William McNeil, Robert DeNiro Sr., Caldwell Brewer and poet Robert Duncan. They turned down a scheduled show at MOMA because they recognized that the Top Floor Gallery more closely resembled their own philosophy which the NAZI called degenerate - 'DERSTVRM'.

The irony is 'The Establishment' of San Francisco attacked the artists of the salon in the same way the NAZI did. Our last exhibit was entitled "Disposable Art" the art in this exhibit along with the building was demolished by the corporate establishment as represented by the Arts Commission for a parking garage for the Symphony Hall.

Just like tearing out the Reflection Pool at City Hall, San Francisco has lost all claims to celebrating and understanding where art and politics intersect. The architect placed the Reflection Pool at City Hall in front of the Mayor's Office so that mayors would reflect on their responsibility to the public, most importantly to the poor and homeless who otherwise have no access to water. Public fountains from Ancient Rome to Paris to San Francisco were and are essential to public health. Now San Francisco's Arts Commission who fronts for the corporate elite relishes their power and restrictive fascist ideology by throwing artists into the streets along with the elderly, veterans, battered women, homeless gay youth, people with HIV/AIDS and the poor.

It had been explained to me by Mark Denton, the new Director of the Neighborhood Arts Project—essentially a representative for the oligarchy imported from Los Angeles—that as long as I supported the preservation of the 330 Grove building, I was out of a job. Breath …

It turned out that Sam Stewart, vice-president of the Bank of America, was a major political supporter of Mayor Moscone, and he wanted the Grove Street properties demolished. He wanted the land so he could build a parking garage for the new Performing Arts Center going up one block away, across from the Opera House. In short, his political clout had resulted in the unethical and possibly illegal condemnation of housing on the 300 block of Grove Street through federal dollars.

The Pride Foundation, radical artists, members of the City's Black community along with citywide preservationist organizations had been fighting this attempt to confiscate low income HEW rehabilitation housing for the Hoi Polloi. Paul Hardman, President of The Pride Foundation, couldn't see turning this great building over to this kind of blatant extravagance. And remember, Harvey had said the building had a soul in his Hope speech. At the time, it had felt like we were winning this fight.

Unfortunately the oligarchy of San Francisco wanted its old world entertainment, no matter the cost to the average citizen. Our precious City by the bay was being ravaged just like the trusting Roman Emperor Augustus was poisoned by his Empress Livia. We were in deep trouble. But who was our Livia? Was it really Supervisor Feinstein or was it someone far more important than this self-serving ambitious politician? All roads seemed to lead to Rome—or is that Blums? Mr. Blum I think is her fourth husband; this one is deeply involved in real estate speculation and had a titans' future in weapons manufacturing which suits Feinstein's personality to a bloody fault.

I watched Harvey's face as he rearranged some papers. I wondered if he had seen the satirical cartoon in the Chronicle's gossip column with a carton of milk representing the Community Center being attacked by fraud. He looked up and said, "Hi, Lee. What can I do for you?"

I needed to know what was really going on, but first I had to soften the blow. I thanked him for nominating me for commissioner of the Open Space Commission created by Proposition J, and thanked him for serving at Pride's Thanksgiving Day homeless dinner at 330 Grove yesterday.

Given the massive deaths in Guyana, the dinner was somewhat morbid. I wore a clear plastic holder around my neck that contained a package of grape Kool-Aid with a tiny white skeleton in memory of the good people murdered by the absurdity of Christian Soldiers. We spoke about the wave of emotions ranging from joy at winning the Briggs Initiative on Tuesday to all the recent deaths.

Then I told Harvey I had a call from Earl Moss. I asked Harvey pointblank if he was selling us out. He said that it wasn't a sellout, but that he was considering voting against the preservationists "as part of a package of vote swaps I am negotiating with the mayor."

If Harvey voted with the administration on the demolition of the City of Paris and the Pride Foundation Center, since Dan White had resigned his position on the board, they would have the six vote majority they needed to control the city. I reminded him that he had campaigned on a preservationist platform. "Remember your campaign slogan 'Harvey Milk Versus the Machine?'" He just stared at me as I continued. "The Victorian Alliance has actively supported you. The City of Paris is their pet project." I didn't like where this conversation was going so I moved on to the next topic.

He had originally supported The Pride Center at 330 Grove Street. I asked him why I heard he was now supporting the squirmy lawyer Walter Caplan with a neo-left wing attempt to take the Gay Community Center away from the Pride Foundation. He said, "Paul Hardman. That's why. He's too old world, too out of step." Yet it was Paul Hardman as executive director of the Pride Foundation who would be down in the basement with a wrench fixing sixty-year-old plumbing and twenty minutes later he was discussing politics with city officials, or bailing kids out of jail who were too visible on Polk Street neatly resolving these issues without breaking a sweat. This man was to old world?

I reminded Harvey that there was a FBI investigation going on concerning the H.E.W. and the illegal condemnation of the 300 block of Grove Street and that fraud had allegedly been committed. According to Paul Hardman, the mayor was being "looked into" by the federal government for possible involvement.

Harvey and I never had a loud argument. We preferred to agree to disagree, yet somehow this conversation was different. Harvey had tasted power and it was to his liking.

I had supported Harvey since his first campaign. We had been in street brawls together during the police strike, fighting off punks in The Castro. We didn't always agree but at least we were, until now, on the same side. We were always candid and direct with each other. I had seen him get real hot under the collar but never with me. After all I am a princess, not a politician.

I do vividly remember one yelling and screaming Queenly debate he had with Paul Hardman in the Top Floor Gallery. Paul successfully procured Supervisor Dan White and Supervisor Gordon Lau's vote to give the Pride Foundation the $375,000 in grants earmarked for the Gay Community Center. This was a shock to Harvey and to Supervisor Feinstein, who had become accustomed to having her Danny Boy's vote in her breast pocket. Harvey didn't want Paul Hardman to continue to control the Community Center. It was too powerful a position to fall into the hands of conservatives in the community. Harvey never recognized that Paul, actually a Republican, did not push his personal politics at 330 Grove. The center had a strong democratic process and everyone was welcome. We did not play partisan politics. Harvey was simply wrong on this issue and it seemed clear that someone he knew had tried to commit fraud regarding the Pride Foundation and the grant allocations.

I felt that the city was big enough for all of us to do what we did best. Our true strength was in our diversity. It was not in any one political corner but in all of them. The only true common thread that ran through the so-called gay community was our oppression. If these queens couldn't get it together and stop bickering over who would be Queen of the May, ultimately we would all lose.

Paul Hardman had performed tremendous work for the community. Harvey felt he was obsolete only because he was a Republican. I could tell Harvey was holding his temper, hoping that I would come around to his position. I did influence a sizable block of votes in his home district #5 and my home district #6 for Carol Ruth Silver. I explained to Harvey that as the first elected openly gay official in San Francisco it was his duty not to involve himself in any politically embarrassing situations. He felt he had his act covered. I tried to convince him he didn't. Paul and Harvey were like two stage queens fighting over the same new dress.

I promised to bring him documents on Monday morning that would explain the entire situation concerning Grove Street. I told him that he would be getting angry phone calls about his vote reversal on the City of Paris demolition from many of his base supporters.

I was stunned. Harvey had promoted the concept of "District Elections." He and Dan White were part of the first crop of representatives from their new districts. Now he didn't believe White's district deserved its own representation. That was not only hypocritical but made him out to be no better than Dianne Feinstein. I just looked at him. He knew the look. Was Harvey now creating a new machine, the "Gay Politically Correct Machine?"

To me, Harvey was fucking up. He relied too much on Mayor Moscone for strength. In turn, Moscone wanted too much from Milk. They were not behaving strategically with all the opposing forces in City Hall. They were not wise enough in the San Francisco homeboy political arena to play the game well. Not that Moscone wasn't a expertly polished politician from his leadership work at the state level. He was, but this wasn't Sacramento, and in this new alliance his timing was incredibly vulnerable. They moved too quickly to solidify power. Harvey took an enormous risk in his alliance with Mayor Moscone for political power and in the end it got them both murdered.

The quaint political problem of Dan White and his Hot Potato franchise on

Pier 39 wasn't being properly handled. White was unable to make ends meet financially on his government salary, so he abruptly resigned in order to open up this business, never stopping to consider how upsetting this would be to the constituents who had supported him in the first election by district. I suggested Harvey just give him his position on the board back. "Stop poking sticks at mad dogs," I said. "Dan White is a weak-minded little man who was far more dangerous on the outside. Put Dan in your debt, make him owe you. We need to win over these right wing-idiots, not polarize them any further." Too late now!

Danger was everywhere. There were rumors of people dropping like flies since Jonestown. I told Harvey what I had heard from COYOTE, yet I was talking to deaf ears. Harvey was determined to support the mayor and keep his nemesis Dan White off the board. I looked at him and there was uneasiness. "You need to be careful that they don't blow your head off and blame it on Jonestown," I said. "Things have been crazy around here all week."

I wanted some eye contact. I had worked too hard for his election to watch him throw it out the proverbial window so he and his neo-Gayourgeoisie lefties could be grant junkies kissing the ass of every foundation and government agency in their new Rolodex for money and power.

"It's just politics, Lee." He wanted that sixth vote. I could see it in his eyes.

"I love you, Harvey. I will see you Monday morning around eleven. Okay?"

"Okay, Lee. Thanks for the flowers."

The rumors were spreading. The mayor had been threatened by phone and police were stationed in front of the Mayor's Office. I watched them as I descended the glorious stairs. I would love to stage a fantasy drama under this great dome someday. The acoustics were incredible. I could hear echoes of Othello lamenting his fatal error. My musings were cut short when as I remembered that there were more than a thousand dead in Guyana. I felt nauseatingly uneasy. I wanted to crawl under a rock.

I bumped into Pride Foundation Attorney John Wahl as I was leaving City Hall. He was representing the victims of the People's Temple Massacre. He was working with the San Francisco Council of Churches to find the poor souls a burial site. We embraced on the steps in the cool afternoon breeze. As he walked away, I reflected on what a good man John was. He was always there to help people in need. It's good to know that a true Christian could be very much like a true Pagan.

I always felt so close to love, so full of life, yet everywhere there was this sense of sickness and melancholy in the air. I felt despair. Downcast eyes and hurried nervous gestures were on the street. My mind was racing as though I was on bad drugs. I needed rest. I could hardly breathe. I walked down the City Hall's steps, crossed the street, and sat on the edge of the glorious Reflecting Pool in the Civic Center.

I often came here to reflect and feed the seagulls and pigeons, to rest and enjoy the splendor of the architecture. I was surrounded with beauty, blue skies, white clouds and beautiful men, but the reflection that was coming from the social climate was not calming. It was dank and morbid. All I could do was weep. I wished the mayor would look out his window and learn from the architect why it is called a Reflection Pool.

Even the victory over the anti-gay Briggs Initiative didn't lower the level of the apprehension I felt in the city. My street sense told me something rotten was in the air. I learned a long time ago to pay attention to my inner voice. I was now on full alert. I had told Harvey he was making a huge mistake and needed to pay attention to the signs. He replied, "You're either in or out, Lee. You work with us or you won't work at all." It was disgusting to hear this from Harvey. He had crossed a line.

When I left him I wondered how he could possibly join forces with Dianne Feinstein et al. He never liked her or her lapdog Lizard People. Now he was voting with her for personal power. I was depressed. I had to do something. I was emotionally drained but I was determined to make Harvey see my point. I went back to my office and collected all the papers I thought would help convince Harvey to support our position.

The artist Adrian who was my business partner in Time Release Records' Tuxedomoon was in Las Vegas for the weekend. He had given me the keys to his studio up on remote Potrero Hill to feed the cat. I caught the #47 Muni Bus and retreated for the weekend. I slept most of the time, despite constant nightmares and waking with restless, relentless cold sweats. I kept going over and over the details. I had to convince Harvey that 330 Grove Street was the right location for the Pride Foundation Center. Even if the Gay Community Center eventually moved to other headquarters with Harvey's new people involved, 330 Grove along with all of our successful services to the community was our bargaining chip. It was the best way to getting what we needed for the community.

Paul had been making advances by negotiating a trade up for the Masonic

Temple building at Van Ness and Market and the Mayor was interested in talking about this opportunity for his own agenda and to meet our community's needs. The Masonic Temple was a grand and stately architectural monument. It would be a huge asset if it became the San Francisco Gay Community Center.

I continued to argue that 330 Grove had major and unique historic relevance. Artists ranging from Allen Ginsberg, to the Cockettes, the Black Artist Community and 60's musicians performing at the Fillmore rehearsed there. The building could be a tremendous asset for the opera, ballet and Museum of Modern Art; for workshops, rehearsals and even storage. We had to save this building, if not as the Pride Center maybe as an Art & Cultural Center. God how I hated politics, power and greed!

Harvey had convinced me to get involved in his neighborhood campaigns, yet now he wanted to tear down the City of Paris. How could this be? Were we now on opposite sides? None of this made any sense. Or did it? Perhaps, as it states in the Chinese I Ching, it is taken for granted that the powerful always tread on the weak. Maybe Harvey really was selling out. I didn't want to believe this. I couldn't wait till I got back to the Hawaiian Islands and away from all these politics.

Monday morning, November 27, 1978, I got up from my stupefying, drowsy, hazy, restless sleep, brewed strong coffee and grabbed my files. The dreams that night had been wild, full of fighting and arguing. When I ran out to catch the #47, the air was biting cold. I would just about make it in time for my appointment with Harvey.

I wanted my position at the Neighborhood Arts Commission back. We deserved it and I wanted Harvey to stand by his campaign pledges, dammit! This was going to be our showdown. I had told Harvey I would be there around 11 a.m. When I got to Van Ness and Grove, I got off the bus and started to walk toward City Hall. To my amazement I couldn't find my Pride files. Where had they gone? Damn, I must have left them at home or on the bus. Oh fuck! Rather than go back I realized I could go over to 330 Grove and make another copy of the information. I walked across Van Ness Avenue with the Opera House standing beautifully against the blue sky. The wind was brisk, the sun was bright, a gorgeous day. Unfortunately the new Performing Arts Center, on the other hand, looked like a giant slide projector.

I hurried to 330 Grove into The Pride Foundation mezzanine-level office. Jimmy Coker was sitting at Pride V.P. Perry George's desk. I sat opposite at

Paul Hardman's desk. Paul was in Mexico City on a well-deserved rest. I went through his files looking for duplicates of my own information. I called Harvey's office and talked to an unknown woman volunteer. She told me Harvey would be in chambers all day and that she would tell him I was going to be a little late. I received a phone call as soon as I hung up, someone asking for our hours of operation.

I told Jimmy Coker that I would be gone for a few hours after meeting with Harvey. I was going to walk down to the Sentinel offices to meet with Beau Riley, the art reporter for The Sentinel, a weekly gay paper. I decided to call Beau to reconfirm the appointment.

I called and Duke Smith answered. I cheerfully asked for Beau. He said, "Lee, didn't you hear? Harvey Milk and George Moscone have just been assassinated."

"What! Jimmy, someone has murdered Harvey and George! Who killed them? Who?"

"Dan White!" was the astonishing reply. I hung up screaming! Jimmy stared at me like I was out of my mind.

Just then Jim Theis, Pride's Volunteer Coordinator, was running up the stairs yelling, "They killed him, they killed him!" Robert Guttmann came running into the room and collapsed into my arms in tears. The wailing and sobbing haunts me till this day. Phones started clamoring, vibrating anxiously through screams and wails that echoed throughout the building. My nightmare was coming true. I could hear the report coming over the radio. George Moscone and Harvey Milk were dead. Dianne was mayor. The worst had happened. I collapsed into my chair to collect my scattering, shattered thoughts.

Jim Campbell called. Jim worked in a warehouse where Dan White's brother-in-law also worked. Then I called mother at work. Someone else answered her line and asked who I was because they were having an emergency. My Gypsy mother had fallen down a flight of stairs. When they put her on she screamed at me asking what had happened. Yet nothing can describe what has happened.

I felt I must go to City Hall. I still did not believe what I was hearing; I had to see for myself. I went out and walked the short block I had just traversed. As I got to the south entrance the door opened. A body wrapped in white sheets was strapped to a dolly, followed by a second one. I was stunned. It took my breath away. I backed up and fell against a car. I felt weak. I couldn't handle this. Yet I had to handle this. How much time has passed? It seemed like minutes but I guess it must have been hours.

I turned away to catch my breath and saw Joan, the executive secretary of the Arts Commission, looking out the window of her office at 165 Grove. She seemed dazed. Breathe, Lee. Breathe. I walked around to the front door of this newly made charnel house. I saw mourners with familiar faces collecting on the steps, hugging each other. I remember Tahara was there from The Angels of Light. Media were arriving. I announced to the cameras there would be a peaceful candle light march in the evening. It was all I could think to say. I knew there would be. We had done it so many times before.

Harvey Milk Campaign Button. Photogpraher unknown

I noticed that many people were still doing business as usual. The news hadn't reached everyone yet. I could see the revelations on their faces as they began to understand. Businessmen with briefcases marched in the doors, they either didn't know, or perhaps they thought chaos is just the way life is. We just continue marching blindly forward in this world of the living dead.

I went inside and walked up the familiar cold marble stairs to the Supervisors' offices. They were roped off by SFPD. I went over to the door of the Supervisors' public chambers. There was one lone rose where Harvey would have sat for the afternoon meeting, in the spot where he would have been able to cast his sixth vote.

Time itself had changed. I was standing in a mysterious vortex of death and destruction. In my brain all I could think was what would have happened if I hadn't lost my file? What if I had been on time for my meeting with Harvey? Would I be dead? Or would I have been able to stop Dan White? These thoughts sicken me to this day.

I drifted in and out about city hall, and then walked up to Castro Street. Walking always helps me sort out my thoughts and calm my nerves. Today, though, I felt like I was walking in an evil dream.

I bumped into Dorice Murphy from the Eureka Valley Promotion Association at 18th and Castro. She stopped her car and motioned for me to get in. She hugged me. She was always such a stern comfort. We had met the night Harvey stormed into the neighborhood association meeting over the police raid at Andy's Donuts. She was the only one there with the balls to stand up in front of hundreds of queens and scream at them until they shut up. I liked her immediately!

Dorice was eventually instrumental in changing local attitudes about our gay "invasion" of the Irish Catholic community which until that time constituted the majority population in The Castro. She whole heartedly supported Harvey in his successful bid for supervisor. Now she advised me to be careful, saying that this was a dangerous time. She warned me that the maggots would be out picking the political bones off the bodies. Dorice had been actively involved in San Francisco for a long time; she knew how dirty politics could get. I kissed her cheek and thanked her for her heartfelt concern.

I found Scotty Smith, Harvey's long-time lover and partner in Castro Camera. We embraced and started to move toward Market Street. A reporter from ABC approached us. The reporter asked if we knew the victims. We looked at each other with tears in our eyes. We both said, "No." We left quickly. I brought him back to the Top Floor Gallery. Jimmy offered him something to calm his nerves. He lay down in the loft to collect himself. The afternoon became a blur.

Memories of this day are forever shifting in my mind in constant conflict. I'm never quite sure which episode happened when. Later, when I went back to The Castro so I could walk with the marchers to honor the fallen heroes, I wondered where Danny Nicoletta, Harvey's long-time sweetheart, was.

We had marched from The Castro so many times, for so many protests and celebrations. I remember walking to City Hall with Harvey and dozens of supporters the day he was sworn in as Supervisor. How excited we were to be a part of San Francisco history. This time there was no jubilation. No obvious enemy to chant against. No Anita Bryant, no Senator John Briggs. We walked solemnly in the cool evening air. I looked at our army of lovers. I was proud to be one of this army. I loved these men. That's just the way it is. If they want to kill me for it, it won't change a thing. I love men. I love Harvey. I love San Francisco. What would we do without him? What would San Francisco become now?

Like a silent brilliant flame-lit Chinese dragon, we coiled through the streets. When we arrived at City Hall there were other dragon processions arriving from other areas of town. There must have been 50,000 or more people. Edgar Allen Poe couldn't have imagined the heaviness of the hearts in San Francisco that night.

That dark evening, just a stone's throw from the historic memorial being staged under the City Hall dome, at 330 Grove, a team of dedicated volunteers were busy answering questions and talking to people from all over the world.

Meanwhile, it was a madhouse at City Hall. Newly appointed Mayor Dianne Feinstein, Supervisor Carol Ruth Silver along with aides to the late Supervisor Milk spoke on the steps. The always annoying Cleve Jones, who has never stopped feeding off Harvey's carcass, addressed the assembled with words of warmth, love, a profound sense of loss, and his newly found career. Cleve is no Harvey Milk. One testimony after another lulled the night into a sweet, exhausting, bitter melancholy.

By the end of the night everyone was singing traditional songs and hymns led by Sylvester and Joan Baez. I stood at the back of the mourners, in the darkness of the library building, with Jimmy Coker known affectionately as my sister Princess Ann. We looked over the candles of the sweeping spectacle, sickened.

As the mourners stood drenched in tears, wax dripping on their hands, they gazed into an uncertain future silhouetted against magnificent architecture. Covered with pastel clouds, the moon lit up the sky. It was an instant spiritual cathedral, the kind of theatrical event Harvey would have loved. I walked off into the night with Jimmy Coker, heading back to 330 Grove and the Top Floor Gallery.

The phones didn't stop ringing. Amid threats of violence from fascist sickos, volunteers answered questions the best they could. We really didn't know what had happened but we were listed in the yellow pages as The Gay Community Center so our phones just rang and rang. Most people were outraged but some, mostly identified as "Christians," were overjoyed that a fatal blow had been struck.

Gay men and women from all over the world called us. They were freaked out and crying, often just wanting to talk to anyone from inside their deep closets. A feeling of helplessness was everywhere. Radio, television and print media reporters from all over the planet flooded our lines. They wanted to know what had happened. They wanted to have us confirm or deny the many rumors that had been spreading. They wanted to know who did what to whom. Once again Harvey had placed us on the world stage. I had to get out. I had to be with people. I needed to reconfirm life.

I was haunted by other memories as well. I had been present the night Robert Kennedy was assassinated at the Ambassador Hotel on June 5th, 1968. I had been elected President of the Young Americans for Robert Kennedy, but after that night I dropped out of politics completely. The memories were too painful. I just don't trust political people yet somehow Harvey had convinced me to get involved with his campaigns. I loved Harvey's spunk. "It'll be fun," he assured me. And everybody knows the Princess loves to have fun.

I hit the streets and got a sandwich from Pérez at the back door of the New York City Deli. She told me she had screamed out the window of her flat when she heard the news, wondering where I was and fearing I was dead. I ate for the first time that day. Somehow I ended up in front of The Mint, a cocktail dive on Market Street. The artist Ruby Zebra saw me staring off into space. He came outside and dragged me in for a brandy. It was the first drink I had had in maybe a year since I had gone Calistoga, the first sparkling water to hit gay bars. Just like with Robert Kennedy, I knew everything was now changed. Nobody could fill Harvey Milk's shoes even though he may have been getting ready to discard the old pair he was wearing himself.

On November 7, 1978, we had gone to the polls and defeated the anti-gay initiative brought about by State Senator John Briggs. On November 18th, the Jonestown tragedy occurred. According to reports, the Kool-Aid massacre had lasted throughout the weekend. On Tuesday the 21st of November, the first count of the dead was placed at 500, but it kept growing. The streets were in a panic, filled with paranoid stories of conspiracy. This had all been barely 10 days ago.

By November 23rd, Thanksgiving Day, George Moscone had received two death threats from people claiming to be from the People's Temple. On Friday, the day I heard from COYOTE that more death was on the way, I met with Harvey and told him what Margo had said. The death count had reached 780 and the public feared the killing would start here in the City. The Jonestown Kool-Aid poisonings had introduced into our psyche the possibility of death squads. It had been reported by the San Francisco papers that the Reverend Jim Jones had an elite team of assassins who would go around the country to finish the dirty job by eliminating the remaining flock. There was suspicion they might go after any political enemies that Jones may have had.

A rumor from the president of COYOTE, Margo St. James, the well-known

Mistress of Prostitutes or, as they were becoming known, "Sex Workers," was being quoted everywhere. One of her girls had apparently slept with a police officer who told her that the police had uncovered a plot, inspired by the death of Congressman Leo Ryan during his Jonestown visit, to kill some elected officials. I called Margo on Friday after talking to Earl and she confirmed this rumor, the same one I brought to Harvey that day. All of this needed to be taken seriously. The code word for this potential plot was "White Knight." By Sunday morning, the 26th of November, the day before the assassinations, the death count in Guyana was up to 910. Could there really be Death Squads coming in San Francisco, the City of Love ...?

On Sunday, a man named Don Horanzy from HUD/HEW, who had been introduced to the Mayor by State Assemblyman Art Agnos, accepted Mayor Moscone's offer to replace Dan White on the Board of Supervisors. They set a press conference for 10:30 am. That evening KCBS news phoned Dan White and asked him for his reaction to Moscone's decision to appoint someone else to his seat. I did not have a television up on Potero Hill and had slept through all this weekend drama.

In Dianne Feinstein's court testimony she had called White on Monday morning and confirmed he was not going to get his job back.

Supervisor Dan White, the accused assassin, was a former San Francisco police officer and fireman, qualified in some minds to be that "White Knight." Rumors of CIA plots placing Supervisor White in Guyana two weeks earlier were spreading on the streets. No doubt, all other conspiracy theories were tied in from President Lincoln to the Symbionese Liberation Army. San Francisco has certainly had its share of bizarre press. Now, a panic engulfed the city. The press would have a field day with this.

Checkmate for the Press Machine ... New Political Board

I spent the entire night of November 27, 1978, on the streets mourning with friends and the grief-stricken. People were sitting in doorways of most buildings, from the Castro to City Hall. I stopped and talked with as many as I could. I walked back and forth again and again, walked and walked among people, young and old who wanted to stay outside. They just couldn't face going to bed. I could not face this new horrid dream either.

On street corners were clusters of mourners: gays, straights, Blacks, hippies, the Chinese, the Mexicans, the Irish, and the Italian-Americans who had lost one of their own. The rich alongside the poor, we were all shocked and we all mourned together. San Francisco had received a mortal wound. The City was in a state of shock: could this be my sleepy romantic fishing village on the California coast where no one locked their doors at night and where people slept in the parks on warm autumn nights? We continued to talk to each other in the hope of understanding. Some felt the need to share and purge their memories, others to pray, and some to weep.

I finally got back to Grove Street early in the morning. I climbed the three long flights to my loft. I was so tired my body was shaking from raw nerves. My eyes were black, blue, and crimson red from lack of sleep combined with the raw pain of crying. I could hardly see my way as I walked through the gallery. Jimmy Coker, aka "Ann," was still talking on the phone. Give that gurl a bottle of vodka and he could stay up for an eternity. I waved at him and went on to my loft. As I lay my head down, I searched my spinning thoughts to find a glimmer of hope, some precious jewel to take into my dream world; something from what I had learned on the streets that would allow me to sleep in screaming peace.

What did I really know? I knew that I had loved Harvey very much and I would miss him, and that we were in a lot of trouble, I also I knew that he had spent his last night on this planet in the arms of an absolute angel, a beloved member of our inner family who loved him dearly, then passed on at the peak of his vital energy. This I knew, this I would have to learn to live with. I passed out.

PLUNGE TO POWER IN A SHALLOW POOL

The following morning over black coffee, Jimmy started discussing the horrid and suspicious events of the preceding 10 days. We continued to discuss them for years to come.

We found much emphasis was being placed on the slaying of gay Supervisor Harvey Milk. But this was not, in my opinion, a singularly anti-gay act. I believe that it was Mayor George Moscone who was the primary target of the assassin's bullets.

The long-time bully Dan White murdered Harvey Milk in cold blood in the most inhuman way. He did it, not solely because of any particular political differences they had, although they had many. He did it simply because he didn't like the fag man. Yet at the same time, he wasn't vehemently anti-gay either. That's why I believe Mayor Moscone was the intended target.

Dan White pledged in his election campaign to, "Eradicate the malignancies which blight our beautiful city." Interestingly, Dan White did have a gay aide and he did contribute one hundred dollars to help defeat the anti-gay Briggs Initiative.

He was the only Supervisor to vote against gay rights legislation until Dianne Feinstein vetoed Harry Britt's Gay Rights Bill from the Mayor's Desk. Feinstein, bidding to become Mondale's vice president, said on "Good Morning America" that the San Francisco Gay Community needed to grow up and tow the line. Yes, she did.

The questions that remain are: Did Dan White act alone, and who ultimately profited from this grisly act? In Warren Hinckle's book "Gay Slayer", the author and columnist from the San Francisco Examiner asks why no one from the gay community has ever come forward to challenge the established verdict on the conspiracy issue. In his book Hinckle draws links between San Francisco insiders and the San Francisco Police Department's involvement in some sort of covert activity that may have caused Supervisor White to take the law into his own hands. This corresponds with the rumor related by Margo St. James days before the murders. Although Hinckle repeatedly tried to point out what he referred to as "The Big Lie," not one of the San Francisco papers would print articles written by Hinckle on the trial.

Was there a conspiracy? Perhaps not a conspiracy where a radical social detractor sat at a table and said, "Let's do this." But there was one of spirit. Dan White may not have been encouraged, yet Dan White felt encouraged. He knew the people he would make happy, and they were just the people he needed to have on his side in order to get away with murder.

Dan White saw himself as a knight in shining armor for the New Right. He was the Great White Hope of the anti-Moscone Police Officers Association. He was also aligned with a powerful group of neo-Nazi sympathizers in his home district. White's association with these fascist pigs was public knowledge in The City, and it had became an issue in his campaign for Supervisor, as had his less than honorable discharge from the San Francisco Police Department. Previously, the SFPD had found White unsuitable to carry a weapon.

Hinckle noted that on one occasion a group of right wingers wearing swastikas had attended a San Francisco board meeting carrying signs supporting Supervisor White. What Warren Hinckle didn't write about was that those in the so-called Gay Community who did speak out and who did ask questions, including myself, were threatened, promptly silenced, blacklisted, beaten, and in the case of Robert Opel, murdered. Many suspected all these threats were to prevent anyone from asking or answering embarrassing questions, especially to the new mayor.

The trial of Dan White began on May 1, 1979. He was defended by Attorney Doug Schmidt. Schmidt had based his case on "diminished capacity." He used questionable tactics by referring to Supervisor Milk as a homosexual as many times as he could. He then referred to the admitted assassin, Dan White, as a good family man whose capacity had been diminished by overconsumption of junk food. This dubious argument became known as the "Twinkie Defense."

Many believed that District Attorney Freitas botched the prosecution. Freitas' chief prosecutor, Thomas Norman, who was considered by many to be one of San Francisco's finest attorneys, never called Undersheriff Jim Denman to the stand. Denman, who had been with Dan White for 72 hours after he had been apprehended, had been quoted as finding White, "In sound mind, cold, calculating, and with no concern for what he had done." It seemed too many in the community that Dan White was not only getting away with murder, but that he also may not have acted alone. He never once showed any remorse for his actions.

On May 21st, Dan White was convicted on two counts of voluntary manslaughter. The maximum sentence was only seven years and eight months for killing two elected officials. This sentence was a huge slap in the face of Lady Justice, a slap that could not go unanswered. San Franciscans had been pushed past the point of decency and were about to revolt.

That night thousands of San Franciscans, led by the city's outraged gay community, attacked City Hall. Empress Mayor Dianne Feinstein, lizard lawyer Walter Caplan, and the brave Police Chief Charles Gain were held hostage in Moscone's Office. One hundred and fifty people were injured by self-appointed White Knights of the Bay who joined the police at City Hall. Later that night, the police themselves rioted on Castro Street, clubbing down gays on the sidewalks and in the bars. They had been angered by Chief Gain's orders not to get rough at City Hall, so they took their frustrations out on innocent patrons in the Castro's eateries and nightclubs, proving that even when doing nothing you are never truly safe in a fascist state.

I wanted nothing to do with the riot. When the verdict came in I was walking on Castro and Market toward downtown. David Israel, a local radio personality was running as fast as he could, screaming, "He got away with murder!" I knew things were going to explode. I had tried all week to convince

Supervisor Harry Britt to plan a peaceful demonstration. I finally erupted at his instigating tactics and verbally forced him off the #8 Market bus, screaming that he didn't represent me. I got a round of applause but he got his riot. It wasn't until the following day I realized that the riot was inevitable and served an important purpose.

My brain filled with anger, I walked on down to the abandoned hotel I'd been sleeping in since the death threats had increased to an intolerable number of letters, threatening phone calls and a clandestine message written on a Gay Nazi match book left next to my head while I slept at 330 Grove. Paul had turned all of this over to the police, but I don't know what good it did. I climbed into a room and crashed. I slept for hours. When I woke I had completely spaced out the verdict and the events of the day. I got up and walked down to the Stud on 12th and Folsom.

When I got there no one was in the bar. The place was dead. I thought it strange that nobody was at the Stud so when I saw Maya behind the bar I asked her, "What's up?" She just shrugged her shoulders. I turned and walked out the door. I stood on the curb when I saw Attorney Mark Renne come running across the street from Hamburger Mary's. He called out, "Lee, hurry. There's a riot going on. You better get your ass off the streets."

We ran as fast as we could back toward the hotel. As we got there three squad cars pulled around the corner. I opened the door to the hotel as the police were getting out of their cars. Mark went in another direction and I ran like hell to the top floor. I went up the hatch and out over the roof, down a ladder, over another roof and down a fire escape. I slid under a window ledge under the fire escape, curled up in a ball, trying to fade into the darkness. I could hear sirens in the distance and the approaching roar of a crowd, an army of lovers seeking revenge. I remembered the stories of Anne Frank. Will people ever learn? This is not how The Princess likes to spend her evenings.

In Randy Shilts' book The Mayor of Castro Street, he relates a story told to him by a neighbor. The neighbor asked, "You know why Harvey died a fag's death?" "No," Randy replied. It was "Because he got blown away! Ha, ha, ha …!" Yet, why did Randy Shilts, who I had allegedly respected as a journalist for his great contributions to the gay community, never mention Paul Hardman or The Pride Foundation, The Gay Community Center, The Sixth Vote, Jonestown and the scandalous events that led up to the assassination of Harvey Milk in his book? Did The Machine edit his brain or just his book? Actually, I know it wasn't his brain. He had already failed the community in his blatant omission regarding any revelation of the relationship to the cabal around Harvey's Machine and those who tried to steal the HEW Funds for 330 Grove. Why?

Another story of the riot was Ruby Zebra's, an avant-garde artist from the postmodern nihilistic punk world. Ruby was cosmically instrumental to that segment of the art community. He saw no hope for the human system of justice for anyone. I remember seeing him at the Sacred Art exhibit, a Hula Palace Salon, sitting on the floor in a corner surrounded by fresh eggs and broken glass, illustrating the fragility of life. His presentation was so gentle, yet still reeked of danger.

When I saw him the day after the White Night Riot, I found out there was another side to his character. He told me he was one of the first to be on the top steps of City Hall before the riot. He claimed to have actually started the riot when he threw a brick through the gilded pontifical doors of the ornate Beaux Arts Hall. He said he stuck his head through the broken glass cursing the police and spitting on the floor.

The Marquee, our nickname for artist Jim Campbell, spelled like the billboard but another royal title, nonetheless was on the steps at that time as well. He witnessed Dianne come out on to the balcony to try and calm the once adoring, familiar crowd. The crowd kept screaming, "Dianne and Dan! Dianne and Dan" over and over again! He then saw a rock thrown by someone flying toward the balcony.

The Marquee said that Chief Gain, instead of pushing Her Loathsomeness over the rail, actually grabbed her by the waist and pulled her back into the Mayor's office with such force that she doubled over. Her normally stiff hair flew like the Bride of Frankenstein. People were screaming "Throw her off, throw her off" because many blamed her and the District Attorney for the outrageously lenient verdict.

The crowd continued screaming, "Dianne and Dan! Dianne and Dan" over and over again!

Ruby told me that anybody that could get that close to Dianne and not kill her deserves to be used and discarded as Chief Gains ultimately was when she immediately ousted him from office. Not much of a thank you for saving her miserable, greedy, self-entitled life.

"Dianne and Dan, Dianne and Dan" The chant was spreading.

Jimmy Coker told me he noticed there was an organized group of unidentified provocateurs in green windbreakers. They moved through the crowd and Ann noticed that wherever they roamed the riot broke out. The Marquee noticed them too, intuiting that they might have been police in disguise, working to instigate violence and give themselves the opportunity they have been seeking for a long time: to kill faggots. Ann went back to 330 Grove and called Supervisor Britt. He spoke to scumbag Walter Caplan and offered any help they thought we could perform from the gallery. Moments later, fourteen police cars were laid to waste in fiery rubble. To Ruby Zebra, my gentle artist friend, this was a beautiful sight.

Feinstein Flyer by Lee Mentley

What had happened to my loving city? I abhor violence in any form. I feel guilty when I step on a roach or brush off an ant and yet all my life I have been avoiding violence while looking down the barrel of a gun. I am glad I avoided this riot but soon I understood why it had to happen. I was so thankful that Gain was a benevolent Chief of Police. For many in the City, in light of a misguided and bigoted judiciary and to protect the memory of fallen martyrs, this riot was the only route left to defend their humanity. It was all anyone could do.

GOOD PAWNS US ALL, ANOTHER NEW FAUX GAME

Harry Britt, a Socialist ex-minister, whatever that means, had been appointed to Harvey's vacant Supervisor's seat by the new Mayor. Mayor Feinstein had handpicked this man over the overwhelming objections of the community who felt that Harvey's aide, Anne Kronenberg, was the most appropriate candidate to carry on Harvey's legacy.

Harvey had left a letter designating who he would like to succeed him if his fears ever came true. Anne Kronenberg was number one on the list. Britt was also on the list, coming in at number five. Feinstein, however, could never tolerate a strong woman on the board. She was much more comfortable with the submissive personalities that sucked up to her and Kronenberg was no suck-up. Britt was one of the "politically correct" control freaks and a neoliberal-socialist so I believe with good reason that she offered him the job to divide the community.

Now that she had what she always wanted, we knew that her Mayoress was polarizing the community in an endless quest for Power. She did a good job turning the "gay political" world upside down. She then went on to tell the Ladies Home Journal that gays would have to learn that their private behavior was considered obscene and that they would have to live within certain boundaries. She was already planning her national agenda; this woman wanted to be President. She was a candidate made in Hell, a Republican disguised as a liberal woman. She was more dangerous than the Reagans.

Obviously, Dianne is no friend of mine. I dubbed her "The Ayatollah Feinstein." Once, I made a flyer depicting her as the Iranian Ayatollah, whipping the gay community into shape. The poster was mentioned in the next issue of Newsweek. Not knowing the source, she told me she was livid about the flyer while I was in her office at a meeting with the presidents of the neighborhood associations. I had overheard her ask Del Dawson, a constant lackey for the Mayor, who was with me at the meeting, to help her find out who had created the Ayatollah flyer. I said, "I can tell you who did it—I did!" Dawson grabbed my arm and pulled me out of the office. I started laughing.

Her political maneuvering made sense to me now. Mayor Feinstein had planted Dawson on the Pride Foundation board to help sabotage Paul Hardman. That's why he pulled me out of the Mayor's Office as fast as he could. He was afraid she would ruin him, and she eventually did. Years later Princess Ann told me he died alone and rejected atop an old heap of rubble; although he'd done all her bidding for years, he was still ultimately screwed over by Dianne, living as more or less homeless on the top floor of a failed community center where he eventually died. Sounds like karma to me.

Speaking of dramatic exits, this wasn't the last time I would be thrown out of City Hall because of Feinstein. Not long after this episode, we started a recall petition that had made the ballot, I was descending the grand stairs as Dianne was arriving with entourage I started screaming "Recall the Bitch!" Her security and my attorney escorted me out of the building.

I believe that for different reasons, both Feinstein and Harry Britt counted on this riot to further their own political agendas. Feinstein, as I have said before, was a candidate made in Hell. She only had to keep her mouth shut, let the police thugs do their thing, and then she could swoop in, falsely save everybody, and win over the gay community. She would enslave us with her new police chief and she would tear us apart politically with the Britt appointment. Ultimately it was Feinstein who tore down 330 Grove. The community did not have a center for the next 30 years. What amazes me most is that the same political queens still support this morally worthless sack of fascism and her sister Pelosi. When was the last time either of these two women did anything for the people of San Francisco beyond ushering in the corporate take over?

Swept along in the drama of the moment, Harry Britt needed a scene to flex his new political muscles, to get himself a life, and to establish his territory. He eventually had his chance on the night of the riot when he threw himself into the fracas on Castro Street and placed his body between the police and the community. It was his shining moment, the one he had planned for all week long in his quest for power. Now he would be electable. It was too bad he didn't use his newfound muscles to have a more responsible reaction to this tragic verdict than a planned political riot necessary as it was.

That is not to say that the San Francisco community owes anybody an apology for the angry events of the White Night Riot. The people rioting in the streets were expressing an outrage that was a millennium in the making. They were no longer going to be easy marks. They would fight back and they would kick ass again and again. That is, until some Gayourgeoisie time passed and they became submissive all over again questing for normalcy. Whatever that is?

It is a mistake, however, to think that this was exclusively a homosexual reaction. When he was in the California Assembly, Mayor Moscone was a champion of civil rights and the immigrant minorities of the city's diverse districts had deep respect for the Honorable Mayor. They were all present to register their protest. The young and the old, men and women, gents and ladies, expressed their outrage. Some threw stones, some bottles, and some set fire to cop cars on that extraordinary night.

The media, however, chose to emphasize the Harvey Milk/Gay angle and so that's the way it played in national press. The media has a hard time expressing reality. It is far easier to go for the outrageous sound bites and fast images of so-called flagrantly violent "Gay Men" than delve into the real target of Dan White, Mayor Moscone.

The riot was a necessary reaction to San Francisco's authoritarian oligarchy that controlled our precious democracy. It became inevitable because of a jury of who knows whose peers that allowed an unrepentant, admitted murderer to go free. It has happened to homosexuals so many times before. Somehow, this was the last straw.

Ruby Zebra was simply the first to shatter the thin veneer. Cleve Jones tried to stop Ruby, screaming that, "Harvey would not have wanted it this way." Knowing that Cleve Jones was perpetually wrong, the Marquee countered that "Harvey loved theater of this magnitude."

Harry Britt pretended to calm the crowd he had actually riled up by telling them they "were acting like heterosexuals." It was the only moment of levity that night. Harry latter denied the comment, but as the Marquee said, Britt should stop being ashamed of his words and claim them. After all, it's the only clever thing he ever said that night.

Harvey would have claimed those words. Harvey was a scrapper who enjoyed a good street brawl. On different occasions, I had busted up several punks and their cars with Harvey on the streets in the Castro. Harvey always fought back. Ruby responded, "Fuck Harvey Milk. I'm doing this for me. I want justice! Kill Dan White! Kill Dianne and Dan!" Many were disappointed they hadn't.

The following week Ruby spent his breakfasts at his South of Market flat with the boys in blue from downtown. Years later when I saw Ruby on the streets of Hollywood, walking past Ron's Records, he pretended not to know who I was or who he was. Those must have been some interesting breakfast meetings with The Man. Another one silenced by the system.

My friend Robert Opel attended Dan White's trial on a regular basis. He was furious with the courtroom procedures he witnessed. He told me he was going to expose the system that let Dan White get off so easy. Robert Opel was sure there was a conspiracy of some sort. I asked him if he meant complicity or if he actually meant that people had conspired. He said he knew what and how it had happened and he was going to write a play about his theory. I had to agree with him on all his points.

Robert Opel was murdered in July of 1979, the summer after the assassinations. Opel, best well-known for streaking David Niven and Elizabeth Taylor at the Academy Awards in 1971, owned Fey Way, an art gallery South of Market. His gallery was dedicated to erotic art. He was a fun-loving radical who employed shock as a tool. He opened minds to the sexual revolution. He was once arrested for dressing as a six-foot-tall Mr. Penis at a Los Angeles Gay Parade. He eventually fled to San Francisco in 1976 after serving four months in the Los Angeles County Jail for stripping nude in front of the Los Angeles City Council and placing his hand on the shoulders of Police Chief Ed Davis as they debated over nude beaches.

Now Opel planned to employ his inexhaustible talent as a writer-performer with a dramatic expose on the assassinations to be presented at the Gay Freedom Day Celebration in 1979. It was to be called The Execution of Dan White. They were going to hang Dan White at the conclusion of the living art piece, "like it should have been done to the bastard, in the first place." Opel told me he received tons of threats. He was told to not do the play or he would have to pay the price. He ignored the threats, indulging in Angel Dust to stimulate his gray cells.

I had a theory early on that Angel Dust was a government plot to destroy the minds of hairdressers. Personally, I had the misfortune to be caught off guard at the opening night of Divine's musical earthquake Heart Break of Psoriasis. I was standing with Harvey Milk and Tom O'Horgan at intermission when they passed me what I thought was regular marijuana joint. I got so stoned that the next day when I saw the bad reviews I thought the critics hadn't seen the same spectacular show I had. I never smoked another one of those awful dusted joints and no one was allowed to smoke dust or do hard drugs at The Hula Palace. Opel, however, seemed to flower creatively under Dust.

Opel said he even received direct threats from members of the Gay Freedom Day Parade Committee itself. That was no surprise to me. The artists from the Top Floor Gallery had to physically fight off the Gay Freedom Day Parade Committee to protect the San Francisco Arts Commission's award winning, one-of-a-kind flags made by artists from Eureka Noe Valley Artist's Coalition, The Hula Palace, and Gay Freedom Day community volunteers in Top Floor Gallery.

These remarkable flags had flown at the San Francisco Civic Center UN Plaza surrounding the once great Reflection Pool on Gay Day 1978. Unbelievably, the Parade Committee tried to take credit for and own the Rainbow

Flags. Later, Gilbert Baker who could barely finish any project he ever started with was the 1978 co-chair of the Gay Day Decorating Committee would later shamefully claim he created the rainbow flags all by himself, at Harvey's request nonetheless—but the artists knew he was no Betsy Ross!

Lynn Segerblon who was the other co-chair with Gilbert Baker of the Gay Day Decorating Committee, along with Hula Palace artist Robert Guttmann, presented their original idea to the Pride Board of the rainbow flag concept. The Pride Foundation requested and found funding through the Hotel Tax. Lynn was the rainbow artist for Capezio downtown and professionally known as Faery Rainbow Argyle. It was Ms. Faery who, working with others, chose the colors and mixed the dye for one thousand yards of bleached muslin and designed the Rainbow and Rainbow American Flag with a sole star placed within the stripes symbolizing "The State of Consciousness."

More than one hundred artists worked on this amazing project. Stop it Gilbert.

I was extremely concerned about Opel's safety. I went down and spent some time in the Fey Way Gallery with John Anthony aka Harmodious, Earl, and Camille O'Grady. We got so stoned that I wasn't sure if I was actually there or not. I kept trying to get some conversation on the performance piece going, but no one could respond. I left in a daze, as though I had taken acid or something.

The Parade Committee canceled Opel's stage performance without explanation. So, being the radical he was, Opel staged his piece of guerrilla theater on a Gay Freedom Day Parade float near the stone slabs of the fountain at United Nations Plaza.

-S.F. EXAMINER ☆ Fri., Sept. 29, 1978 |

San Francisco Arts Festival awards decided

Top cash award in the fine arts category at the San Francisco Arts Festival — that's $325 — has gone to Elizabeth Bush of Oakland for her watercolor, "Cactus No. 3."

Other fine arts award winners are: Luis Ramirez, Oakland, $300; Lawrence J. Herrea, Oakland, $265; Terry Lim, Oakland, $45; Mary Ann Helmholz, Burlingame, $100; Tom Meisenheimer, San Francisco, $250; Stephen McMillan, San Francisco, $70; Craig Henry, San Francisco, $200; George Poliakoff, San Francisco, $80; Cathleen Daly, San Francisco, $200; Eleanor Rappe, San Francisco, $175; James Bolton, San Francisco, $180; Xavier Viramontes, San Francisco, $165; Dennis Beall, Sausalito, $150; Peter Baczek, San Francisco, $140; Stan Washburn, Berkeley, $125; Terry Woo, Berkeley, $90.

The top crafts award ($350) was taken by Mollie Pupeney of Orinda for a coil-built burnished pot. Other crafts winners are: Andrew Bergloff, Fremont, $75; Diana Flyr, San Francisco, $80; Gary and Virginia Holt, Berkeley, $100; Larry Murphy, Sonoma, $55; Randy Strong, Berkeley, $50; Michael Cohn, Emeryville, $60; Raymond Pelton, Napa, $130; Ann Puski, Pacifica, $68.

Fine Arts merit awards went to Elio Benvenuto, Charles Griffin Farr, James Lawery Jr., Nobuo Kitagaki, Jesse Wetterstein and Beverly Toyu of San Francisco, Ev Thomas of Oakland and Fred Strebel of Emeryville.

Crafts merit awards went to Naomi Stahl of El Sobrante, Vera Allison of Mill Valley, Genevieve Barnhart of Sebastopol and Kent Raibe of Fairfax.

✗ Group merit awards went to the Eureka/Noe Valley Artists Coalition, Metal Arts Guild, S.F. State University Ceramics MFA students, the Alvarado Arts Workshop, the San Francisco Neighborhood Arts Program/CETA, and Bonnie Engel, coordinator of the Moebius Video Competition.

Two weeks later, after a short visit at Fey Way on my way to the Glory Holes on 6th Street, Robert was murdered in his gallery by two career criminals. They blew his head off in what was claimed to be a drug deal gone sour. Robert was with our Harmodious, a sweet handsome young man, and the exotic leather rock artist Camille O'Grady when he was murdered. They were saved from certain death when Phillipino teenagers whose family lived upstairs, rushed down, interrupting the killers. These two gentle souls who were with Opel were threatened repeatedly but testified at the trail anyway. The cover story was they went into seclusion somewhere north of San Francisco but laid low in the city waiting for the trial. The two murderers were apprehended but on three occasions walked right out of the court room. One is now dead and the other is not allowed to have interviews.

Did Robert Opel know something that led to his death? Or, as the press reported, was he a paranoid personality on drugs who spoke out and co-incidentally paid a huge price. Both could be true. And as an interesting footnote, 30 years later his nephew—also named Robert Oppel—made the award-winning comprehensive movie Uncle Bob. (The spelling of Robert's last name was changed in the 1970s on purpose to protect Robert Opel's family in Philadelphia)

I stayed at the Glory Holes all night. On the way back to the gallery I walked right by Fey Way. I glanced in and saw nothing unusual and walked on. When I got to the Top Floor Gallery, Ann told me Robert was dead. I said that was impossible. I had just seen him last night. I called the Sentinel to ask Duke Smith if it was true and he told me what had happened. He also informed me that some of his sources named me as the next fag to get it. When I asked him to clarify his remarks he wouldn't reveal his sources. He advised me to be careful or get out of town.

I went into deep cover as a bag lady. I approached a friend who had contacts within the police department and, at great risk to my friend, safety arrangements were arranged. As President of the Eureka Valley Promotion Association in The Castro, I had to make public appearances. There were four maybe five major threats in all, along with lots of nasty phone calls and letters. Someone did try to firebomb the Pride Center but we fought them off with fire extinguishers. They did manage to damage our phone lines and set fire to an inside dumpster. I would continue to disguise myself as my favorite bag person to get across town, only this time costumes were no longer for fun. I lived like this for over a year, until I moved to Los Angeles in February 1981.

QUEEN'S KNIGHTS TO QUEEN'S PAWNS

Another question I heard over and over again was the possibility that San Francisco Police Officers were involved in the assassinations of the Mayor and the Supervisor.

On the day of the assassination, less than two hours after White pulled the trigger, a one-time member of the Pride Foundation Board of Directors, who was also a San Francisco police officer, arrived at 330 Grove Street headquarters with a hand stenciled tee shirt that read "Free Dan White" with painted bullet holes in it. He had received it that day as a token of affection from some of his fellow SFPD officers. He said it had been given to him amid a jubilation of salutations for Dan White. It seemed to me that Dirty Harry was more than a Clint Eastwood movie.

This was reported in various radio broadcasts right after the murders were committed along with the singing of that favorite Irish tune Danny Boy. Of course this was also denied by the Police Department. There were no tee-shirts presented to the press.

Why was there no adequate inquiry of the assassinations, aftermath, or the trial by the media? When the streets were full of speculation, the kind of music the press usually likes to sing—investigating conspiracies—why was there not a single song to be heard. There was no scrutiny. It was as though the media just wanted everyone to go to the opera and park in the new lot and look the other way.

QUEEN'S KNIGHT TO CBS , NBC, ABC, & KICU-TV CHANNEL 36...,

San Francisco Police Department had its old boy hierarchy dissolved by Mayor Moscone when he appointed Charles Gain, a reform-oriented former police chief from Oakland, as Chief of Police in 1977. Gain reorganized the SFPD to bring strong arm tactics by the police to an end. The buddy system was over. The new chief moved as quickly as he could to integrate the department. He instructed his officers to respect all the minorities in their districts as a direct order from the newly elected mayor. The SFPD did not like this.

Chief Gain was responsible for saving hundreds of people from possible injury or worse, on May 21, 1979, the night of the White Night Riot. It was no secret that the Police Officers Association, the political arm of the department, wanted Gain out and one of their own back in. Later, this would be a requirement for their powerful endorsement of Dianne Feinstein's bid for the office of Mayor of San Francisco. She, of course, complied.

QUEEN'S KNIGHT TO KING'S KNIGHT, CHECK

How did Supervisor Dan White come to be a murderer? Was this really the act of a lone assassin? Was he just a friendly butcher for the homophobic and racist hate-mongers from his home district? Was he truly desperate from stress and suffering from an overdose of junk food as his attorney pleaded? Or perhaps there are even more profound implications to examine?

In our democracy we have peaceful procedures for the resolution of political differences. We elect people to office so that they may represent the people's will or so we are told to believe. George Moscone, Harvey Milk, and Dan White were elected by the people of San Francisco. So how did we lose our civility and crash blindly into chaos, losing not two, but three public sons? Would we make it through this socio-political wilderness?

If we look to the "Be Here Now" philosophy of San Francisco in the Summer of Love that gave birth to the Sexual Liberation and Humanistic Movements of the 1970s, we have to look at the concepts of the San Francisco 1960s philosophy "We are all one. We create our own reality and our own destinies. We are all responsible for the web that holds society together. Through our thoughts we create our culture." Power comes from within. Put a fucking flower in your hair.

In this respect, we all played a part in the fall of the City. Did collective hatred lurking in citizen's hearts reinforced and inspire Supervisor Dan White's sad, sick, depleted psyche.

THE ONE HUNDREDTH IDIOT SYNDROME

Did this pervading attitude help lead White, dripping in sacrificial blood, through the corridors and chambers of San Francisco's City Hall. I believe there was a fatal flaw in Supervisor Milk's decision to support the Mayor against Dan White to get their sixth vote. Their shared petty desire for political power, over a parking lot and a department store stoked their desire to cast an ironic vote with arrogant finality that led to their assassinations by a murderously deranged idiot. I think they call this a perfect storm.

SHAMANISTS FLOWER POWER PAWNS US ALL

What effect does inner motivation have on the creation of society? The guilt of the City, felt during the dirge that followed the season of death, was painful and obvious on the faces in the streets. The people on the buses were silent for days. We all had our own sense of guilt. Harvey himself bore some responsibility for the manner of his death. It's haunting.

On many occasions, among friends and constituents, Harvey would expose his death wish. "Someday I will have to pay with my life, at the hand of some irate bigot. Let the bullet that rips through my brain open every closet door in the nation." After his loss to Art Agnos for the California Assembly he made a tape recording repeating this death scenario. He wanted Attorney John Wahl to have it played if he was ever assassinated. I regularly sent him flowers asking him to stop the brooding. I told him I would send him flowers now, before some idiot killed him. He just laughed. Was he being prophetic, or was he also helping subconsciously to create a Dan White?

Who hated George Moscone and Harvey Milk so much that murder was the result of that hatred? All murder mysteries say "follow the money." So, who profited and who continues to profit from the assassinations? To start, let's reflect that you can now park your car at 330 Grove!

Every event that has attempted to shed light on the circumstances surrounding the soft handling of Dan White has been met with official harassment in the courts and with little help from the criminal justice system. San Francisco Attorney Judge ProTem John Eshleman Wahl, the executor of Harvey's estate, was denied on several occasions motions to retry Dan White for federal civil rights violations for depriving Harvey of his civil rights. Attorney Wahl exhausted all available legal remedies to keep White behind bars. He also tried to keep White from profiting from his crimes.

All protest concerning this crime had been glossed over and neatly covered up. Steve Dobbins, a playwright and director, produced in 1980 the docudrama The People vs. Dan White. Taken directly from the transcripts of White's trial, and from a series of some 160 interviews, Dobbins reveals the official kid-glove treatment White received while in custody.

White's jail cell had its own phone and a typewriter. He was visited by prominent San Francisco politicians including Mayor Feinstein and police officers. He never ate prison food, fearing that homosexual inmates in the prison kitchen would attempt to poison him. This former junk food addict now had his food catered. He had clean sheets in a prison where prisoners are not allowed to have sheets. He was allowed conjugal visits and his wife became pregnant. Some officers from the SFPD set up a million dollar "Mary Ann White Trust Fund" account at Sumitomo Bank on the corner of Stockton and Sutter Streets that would pay off in 18 years to help support his unfortunate prison-conceived child, who was born medically challenged.

Earlier in 1979, "Execution of Justice", another play that explored the nature of the assassinations opened on Broadway in New York City. The playwright Emily Mann explored how autopsy reports had been altered to supposedly spare Harvey's lovers Scott Smith and Danny Nicoletta, and Harvey's family, from further grief. In the play Dan White announces that he was going to shoot Harvey Milk "where the sun doesn't shine." Later, when Attorney Wahl received custody of the clothing Milk was wearing the day he was murdered, he turned it over to Danny and Scotty. Scotty told me that there was no evidence that White had carried out this threat. There was no evidence of bullet holes or blood in his under-clothing ...?

During the run of "The Dan White Incident" written by Steven Dobbins and performed at Fort Mason in San Francisco, some of the actors said they were threatened. Tires were slashed in the parking lot. Bomb threats were received on most nights just before curtain time. Dobbins, fearing for his life, left San Francisco. He went underground to do a rewrite of the play.

He premiered the rewritten version in Los Angeles on January 5th, 1984, at the Pan-Andreas Theater just one day before White was to be paroled. The performance was reviewed by Dan Sullivan in the Los Angeles Times. Mr. Sullivan in his review states, "The play leaves you knowing more about the assassinations, and raises serious questions about the treatment of Dan White." Yet no one in the national media asked any questions. No real attention was given to the play in the press. Can you imagine if this had been a different California politician at the time like Governor Ronald Reagan? How much attention do you think the media would have spent on that scenario?

QUEEN'S KNIGHT GOES TO L.A.

The first official act of Dianne Feinstein's Administration was to ask for the resignation of Police Chief Charles Gain. She then appointed a new chief of police. Upon the department's request, and with the support and approval of the powerful Police Officers Association, Feinstein appointed Cornelius "Con" Murphy as her new police chief.

During the tenure of Mayor Feinstein police brutality complaints increased in all areas of San Francisco. A special Civilian Review Board was set up to handle the increased public outcry for justice and support for those who were now being attacked and brutalized by the SFPD. Yet there was no justice forthcoming. There was no longer a George Moscone, Harvey Milk or a Chief Charles Gain to guarantee the public peace. The Mayor herself carried a loaded gun in her purse.

In October 1984, Mayor Dianne Feinstein sent her police chief to Southern California to meet with Dan White with the hope that White could be dissuaded from returning to San Francisco when his parole ended on January 6th, 1985. The idea that he might return to the scene of his crimes had haunted many San Franciscan politicians. Chief Murphy used all his persuasive powers, but to no avail. No one wanted to push Danny Boy too far. After all his track record illustrated that after a donut or two he kills those who oppose him.

White returned to San Francisco in 1984, joining his wife, a part-time school teacher, and his two small children. A right wing group in Orange County California had offered to finance White should he decide to attempt to return to public office and run for supervisor again. After all, he had omly killed a fag and a nigger lover.

Mayor Feinstein had made it embarrassingly clear that her little Danny Boy was not wanted in his hometown anymore. Mayor Moscone's wife declared the "City was not big enough for them and Dan White." California State Assembly Speaker Willie Brown, on an ABC Nightly News broadcast called White's return, "The sickest thing I ever heard of. Can you imagine Sirhan Sirhan having dinner at the Ambassador Hotel or the White House? Or Charles Manson visiting Sharon Tate's parents, or having brunch with Roman Polanski?"

On October 21st, 1985, Dan White was found dead of carbon monoxide poisoning, an apparent suicide, at his home in San Francisco. No Twinkies were found at the scene.

In the 1990 California Primary for Governor, Dianne Goldman-Berman-Feinstein-Blum, in her best adventure yet into poor taste, appeared in a political commercial featuring herself at her finest moment, as savior of the city of San Francisco after the grisly murders of her political nemeses Mayor George Moscone and Supervisor Harvey Milk. At the same time, when Harry Britt advanced Gay Rights legislation after the assassinations, always remember that Feinstein vetoed that bill.

The Spider Queen shows us all how to eat and grow rich with whatever falls into our webs.

CHECK MATE, NEW BOARD, NEW GAME, SAME OLD SHIT

Breathe

Adrian and HRH Lee. Photo by Daniel Nicoletta

UNMASKING THE MONKEY

Castro Street End
Where Business Persons
Wash sidewalks
In morning suits
To cover up the
Last night smell
Of Crisco, booze & amyl.
To stalk
Exploitation of human need
Into fashionable commodity.

One sassy San Francisco morning Pérez and I, while coming home from a late night, decided not to get trapped by sleep and hit the streets to eat ourselves across the city. Sometimes that's just necessary!

Starting in the Castro with fresh greasy donuts, hot coffee at Andy's Donuts, followed by an eventual lunch with my bookie Itzy at Yee Jung, our favorite Cockette cave downstairs, next to the Universal Cafe in Chinatown with the best ever fresh made Chow Fun!

Our plan: a different treat at each restaurant, bakery and cafe to satisfy a heavy bout of munchies and combat any possible hangover! If you love to eat, San Francisco has a way of enticing your passions along with all sorts of other oral passions.

By afternoon, Pérez and I were turning figurative somersaults in Union Square watching mime Robert Shields do his sweet antics. We ended up at Woolworths. Pérez entered; I followed through the Powell Street entrance to avoid the pedestrian crunch at the Trolley turnaround. We walked straight through the store and ended up in front of the mask counter where we met The Mask Man!

He explained to us that originally the Woolworths Department Store that graced Powell and Market Streets was a series of over 100 shops, specializing in exotic and rare imports from all around the world, ranging from handmade necessities, fashion, foods, and hardware. The mask counter, he proudly noted, was the last remaining concession from the original collection of Barbary Coast shops. All masks were individually crafted and molded by the owner, the father of the Mask Man telling us this story.

While Pérez was figuring out how she could lay him right there for a mask, my eyes kept going to a monkey mask, one that was so form-fitted it completely fit my bald head like real skin. My imagination raced towards nasty. Pérez decided on a white magician mask — and only had to flash her tits. I promptly bought mine with cash. We ran toward the door wearing the objects d'arte that now covered our faces, faces busting out in hysterical laughter.

Pérez caught the #8 Market electric bus. I was eager to get to 14 Isis Street, just south of Market. "I think I'll head back 'South of the Slot' to sleep in my tree." I kissed the White Witch. "Ta Ta. This has been most fun, sweetheart!" Off she went to find, in her words, "that horse of a different color," wearing her mask amongst the buzzing city we called Oz. "You Sleazy Funky Filthy Sick Animal!" she called out to me, her transformed ape.

I grunted off and walked up Market, then straight down 11th Street, south toward Folsom, past ruins that would became the Bank of America world brain. Feeling the mask on my face, I noticed my shadow on the wall of the Coca Cola Building. I realized I looked like an urban gorilla. All I needed was my Patty Hearst pink plastic machine gun. That would be a great neo-punk shadow and poster!

Since everyone in San Francisco had been wearing a figurative mask since the assassinations, it struck me as funny that we were now desperately playfully hiding behind our entertainments. The image of romantic San Francisco itself was now a mask itself. I got to Mission Street, to Howard, to Folsom Street, turned right at the Covered Wagon, walked one short block down past the graffiti wall and Hamburger Mary's. I waved at the Great Goddess Artista, our resident diva who lived in #5 above me at 14 Isis, crisscross from the infamous dance bar, The Stud.

I had kept my art studio at The Hula Palace for salon work, and I wanted to be closer to the action on Folsom. That's why I took this shabby apartment on Isis in the middle of a hideous sex-crime spree that eventually left many men decapitated and mutilated circa 1975. Bodies were regularly found abandoned in dumpsters, vacant lots and in an elementary schoolyard less than a safe distance from 14 Isis. I could have watched these crimes committed from my window seat.

The old apartments located on the corner of Isis and 12th are sleazy 1920s three floor walk-ups filled with leather men. Their inhabitants include Sunshine Johnny, Lou Rudolph, bookies, an ancient alcoholic Spanish immigrant named Roberto and his sometime-lover Guadalupe, plus the one and only divine Goddess of the night, Artista.

Artista's prior incarnation was "Medusa," named after that mythical creature whose looks could kill any unwanted spectator or admirer. In this life Artista was a divine erotic painter, sculptor and often a bouncer at Hamburger Mary's. Artista painted a mural on the roof of 14 Isis before I moved South of The Slot, the metal tracks on Market Street. Artista created an Egyptian love temple with full color representations of Goddess Isis giving birth to the earth, intertwined with the death of Osiris, who was murdered by Seth and re-assembled by Isis, except for his missing penis. We supplied the penises.

By day we sunned our sultry olive-oiled bodies in the industrial sun. By night, from the rooftop temple, we picked up men waiting in the parking lot below, motioning them around to the back stairs. We got their night started with a city view of the Transamerica Pyramid and the gigantic brightly lit Hamm's Beer sign that poured beer into a waiting glass 50-feet-tall all night long. It was our own private Alexandrian rooftop barge, complete with gladiators, slave gurls—and beer!

I kicked open the plywood-covered front door, checked my mailbox, climbed one flight, unlocked the door, walked down the hall to my bedroom, and sat on the edge of the bed. I slowly moved my head down between my knees to stretch my sore neck. I took a deep breath, and slowly lifted my monkey head to lose myself in the mirrors. What a sight!

The mask clung to my head like lubricated rubber, moving perfectly with my face. I knew Michael, my shell-shocked man-friend, was going to love this. At least for 10 lucky minutes. Then he would shoot his load and lose his sense of humor—soon, I'm going to have to dump him.

I decided to wear the mask to dinner. Only in San Francisco can you go to a sit-down dinner as a monkey and have no one actually mention it other than, "How good you're looking tonight, Princess. It must be the mask." Taxi!

The next day I played dress-up with my new persona "The Monkey Man" for my new beau. Adrian—my crazy sister and business partner in Isolation Enterprises-Time Release Records—was having a cocktail party for the new wave band Tuxedomoon, our own Nijinsky, Mr. Winston Tong, and the exquisite Esmeralda from a New Wave duo, Noh Mercy.

Design by Adrian Craig

Adrian wanted a celebration to mark the beginning of Time Release Records. In addition, Winston had just won an Obie award for his one-man show about the inner pains of his Chinese grandmother's torture as a young girl to old woman, entitled, "Bound Feet" at La Mama, an off- off Broadway theater in New York City. It wasn't very often that New York City recognized the artistry of San Francisco-based artists. They would rather be bored in New York than look elsewhere. Winston was so far off-Broadway he might as well have been from another galaxy!

We were just about to start our first "Off the Deep End Tour" of the East Coast, including New York City, Philadelphia, Boston and other cities with Tuxedomoon. It was a truly exciting phenomenon. San Francisco had accomplished the fine art of turning Punk Rock into New Wave with eerie tritone sounds, haunting melodies on violin, and straight soprano sax creating angst blues of San Francisco's frightful nights known as a Tuxedomoon.

We were taking West Coast underclass into the Big Apple. San Francisco was teeming with a new strange creativity in an attempt to put some meaning into the darkness. New Wave Rock Art was emerging with musical groups Tuxedomoon, Noh Mercy, Dead Kennedys, The Offs, The Mutants, Black Flag, The Units, Los Microwaves, and the dramatic, ethereal performance art of Winston Tong. And live onstage painting was being created by Lou Rudolph, the handsome Ambush bartender, son of a mortician, who lived at 14 Isis #9 with the rest of us freaks. The disheveled creatures of the night had changed the nature of music that had arrived from Britain and bounced it back off the West Coast wall. No tears for Disco. An end to all that prenatal shit the Clones clung to as an identity. Something new was happening. An intriguingly devolved day had begun with radical twists on lyrics, a romantic longing for a distant, twisted time, an unattainable point of view dressed in white tie, kid's animal print pastel pajamas, formal hats and dragon tails. If only I could become a day walking vampire, everything would be right with the world! There was plenty to eat if you loved blood.

Adrian convinced me to take a few of these Godzilla Monster groups out on tour. We were opening in New York City at Max's Kansas City and on April Fool's Day bringing this new music to Andy Warhol's Mudd Club. Warhol said he was doing this as a joke on Tribeca groupies, I was sure we would win this round of the long-standing NYC-San Francisco artistic rivalry.

Adrian loved the vampirish scene—speed balls and all—so we went along to protect his back. Adrian had met the French walking-cyber-punk-operatic-tenor from Paris, the amazing Klaus Nome, his devoted Ricardo and the magical Joey Arias. I had seen them with Bowie on Saturday Night Live but it was a surprise kick to meet these goddesses in person on the same stage as our groups. Klaus was a very late Ziggy Stardust gone Dada, a god of the poetic concept of the space between lines. For that extra bump, he traveled around the city with a colorful gang of zombie slaves from Fiorucci's, a trendy boutique for crimes against fashion. Interesting, but for me, I'll wear a monkey mask, please — too much work and too much makeup for the 80s! I could tell they never saw the light of day. I grew to hate the sun. I wanted to become a vampire. It became my newest life goal.

I love New York. I love Manhattan. I was so happy to be back on the grimy streets amongst old friends with a new act.

I read there was an Etruscan exhibit at the Metropolitan Museum where I just knew I had been buried in a prior life. I made a plan to meet a spitfire flamenco dancer Shauna Snowflake at the Met. Over the years we had visited many collections of ancient artifacts to commune with the creative spirits. In 1971, I fell asleep in a sarcophagus after just such an outing. Once discovered, I was thrown to the curb by security. I told them I didn't have to explain myself. I was tired and it was mine from a past life anyway.

One night after Max's, I slipped down into The Bowery to see another new band "The Police." I was enthralled. Their lead singer, Sting, sang his heart out for his supper. Klaus Nomi, Joey Arias and Ricardo were ringside, so it had to be hot. I fit neatly in between. I asked once again, "Now can I become a vampire?" This Police guy worked up such a sweat, a blonde hunk with a brain. Music was back. Kewl!

OH GAWD. Sometimes I get so spaced out and carried away. So ... back to San Francisco and my mask!

I decided to wear the monkey mask to Adrian's soiree. I wanted to see how far I could take this new disguise. I explored many changes. I always have wanted to wear everything. It's just my Gemini nature.

My first idea was to become a Monkey Man bag woman. I love bag women. They give me strength. I will make a proud, big, old, strange-looking bag woman with a monkey face. Fun! Fun!

I ripped into my old steamer trunk and found a body stocking. I wore it with high woolen socks and military boots, over which I wore that Hula Palace 40s floral Sofia Loren drab olive green rayon, with white-and-black poke-a-dots, complete with silver-speckled buttons down to the waist. A Monkey Man's matron's dress for sure or an old Russian woman's! Add an army coat, an Ann-Margret wig, and an army hat. "There now, let's see," gazing into the mirror I went. Well, maybe not. Maybe a shorter wig, more Shirley Booth eats Martha Ray and less Jane Fonda does Annette Funicello!

So in my bag I stuffed blacks, leathers and other decorative accouterments I might want to wear or use later. In a hurry, I grab a leash, a Mao Tse Tung tee shirt, wigs, drugs, water and who knows what else.

Taxi!

I push the buzzer. Adrian lets me in. I could only hear light chatter, the embarrassing sounds of an empty affair. He lived in what used to be an old pharmacy with a second-floor mezzanine. Shit, I was too early. Adrian was cordial, but leery at the dyke-military-monkey-man-bag-woman crashing his party. I wasn't sure if he knew who I was or not, but I was going to play it through. Say nothing, Princess. Only a few people were there, including Adrian's mother and grandmother.

They were having their first San Francisco experience. Oh GAWD: Culture Virgins of the motherly kind. But not after they saw me. Ha! I knew this would be fun. I will just play with them for a while. I walk over and joined the lovely ladies on the sofa. "And how are you, my dears? What have you come as?" Mom and her Mom were a bit unnerved. The buzzer buzzed and broke the uneasiness. A motorcycle dude arrived with Mona and there were a few other boys arriving with them too. Yay! More voices. The music picked up the beat. The party had officially begun.

I excused myself from the Moms and went for the refreshments. I hadn't eaten since last night's dismal dinner. Jimmy Coker—who came as his sister persona Ann in a tailored two-piece, off-white Saint John knit, Pacific Heights I Magnin ensemble with a soft ice-blue blouse—was lurking at the table. He had arrived with Ida, the Serious drag queen. I nudged Ann and in a low grumble, said, "It's ELA, Ann." She raised her luscious eyebrows, "I know who you are Queen—nothing gets past me."

We walked over to the side buffet to sample the treats. Adrian walked up and said, "Excuse me, I don't want to seem rude, but do I know you?" I just loved it. My very own all-knowing sister=buddy actually didn't recognize me! What a moment in my inexhaustible drive for recognition, to be noticed but not known.

I dragged him away and asked if he would keep a secret? She agreed. We stepped into the little gurl's room. I removed my mask. We gurrrlllled it up, then we lifted our spirits with a little toot. We went back to party to confuse the boys and slam dance the night away.

When it was over, I ended-up wrapped-up in the back seat of a taxi with a sexy young blonde number. He told me his name was Golden Rod and he was dressed as a space hero. Well, I've never seen him before, but he is my Golden Hero—at least for right now! As I stepped into the taxi I noticed the driver was Brent from the Cockettes. He promised not to look or at least not too much!

Golden Rod and I went animalistic. A UFO Spaceman and a Monkey Man, cavorting in the back seat crossing the Mission into the now tamed, well-behaved gay ghetto. There was a time where no one would have noticed what I was doing. Now, eyes were everywhere. As I have said before, "I'm not Gay anymore—I'm Just Pissed Off!"

We paid our Daddy Man's fare with a huge tip for not looking, and in our smeared afterglow, we stepped out onto Castro Street, renewed. I kissed my nasty, spent space hero goodnight and headed toward Market Street. What's next, I wondered? The night was just getting started!

I thought of paying a surprise visit to Tommy's Plant Store to scare him pink. He was so delightfully pink. Especially when I got to spank that pretty white butt!

And one of the best kissers on Castro—but mushy love could wait.

I walked up to Market and turned east toward the downtown city lights. I loved seeing the James Dean painting by Kabbaz in the window of Hot Flash. There was a litho-photo of the painting and Kabbaz himself as a print by Crawford Barton, and it was so good! Window shopping while watching my Monkey Man reflection in the glass started to get interesting. Me as a monkey, mixed with James Dean, Kabbaz and Crawford, with lots of neon glam, became "a hero sandwich" of sorts." I liked that thought. It was all so sexy, I could fuck this window.

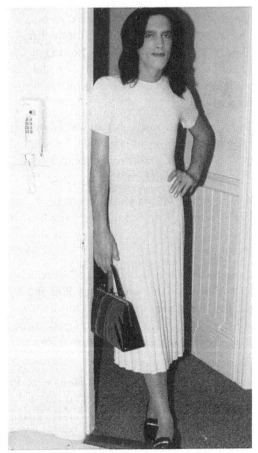

Jimmy Coker. Photo by John Serrian

I walked for blocks, all a-frolic. By this time, I was totally into Monkey Man. I had become Monkey Man! I crossed Market Street, skipped over trolley tracks past Church Street Station, into a Safeway parking lot, and picked up a shopping cart. I threw my bag in it and coasted on the cart to the Goodwill Free Box to see if I could find some new drag—or to see if Crown Prince Arcadia was sleeping in the box. We could smoke a joint. I had heard the Prince had taken over the Free Box and was living in it. Neither turned out to be happening. No exciting new drag or hats—although I did find an interesting frock for house cleaning, a relatively clean polyester pillow, a ratty black handbag with change in it—but no Prince.

I decided to head for Polk Street where, if I was lucky, I could heckle the hustlers I knew but who wouldn't know me. I'd scare off their tricks. Ha! On

I went, into the fray. After ruining a score of nerves of those strolling up one side of Polk Strasse, I then worked the other side down to Le Salon, an old closeted man's porno bookshop and tacky cruise scene, one where married men picked up "straight" boy runaways for quick, so-so not so good sex. Been there, done that! Got 'a eat.

I backed up into a darkened doorway in the alley just around the building and pulled the cart up in front of me to relax and enjoy. I watched a few hot loads delivered behind the dumpster to an old time cocksucker. Love those guys. Eventually discouraged by the minimal action, I walked on to City Hall. By the time I got there Monkey Man had melded.

Monkey Man crawled up the stairs on all fours, embodying the monkey he had become. He hissed, sniffed and growled at the imagined politicians and their sycophants. He glared through the gilded doors, doing monkey dances from another time, on the steps, under the dome, where so much monkey-ing around goes on all the time. He screamed, "Fuck all you bloody greedy bombastic bastards. You Killed George and Harvey!" Monkey Man turned to look toward the plaza and proclaimed, "They have killed The King and The Prince. Long may they live!"

Monkey Man ran down the steps toward the reflection pool, grabbing and pushing the cart as fast as he could run, laughing wildly, howling madly. "You have killed San Francisco, you fucking politically correct bastards! Why don't you just tear out this Reflecting Pool and finish the job on this once-great City!"

I finally stood at United Nation's Plaza where piggish lawyer Wart lived as a respectable human until he was arrested. At last, some justice! I remember the night Sister Ann, on one of her drunken escapades, pissed in Wart's mail slot. I'm sure he never noticed. I think he would have actually like the smell.

Monkey Man panted to catch his breath. Breath … Breathe That's when I discovered Helen.

While still catching my breath, I saw an ancient bag lady lying on the ground. I thought she might be dead. I called to her. No reply. My spirits dropped. Major concern came over me.

I reached down and touched her as she lie on the cold damp pavement. To my amazement, I touched a warm hand. Utterly peaceful, and somehow strangely loving, I had to embrace this warm hand. She had suddenly trans-fixed me. She awoke, rubbing her eyes, and looked up, saying "Hello" in an innocent voice. She told me her name. "I'm Helen."

"Well, hello," I replied. "I know I must look like a monkey, but actually I'm The Princess."

We talked; me in my monkey mask and she in hers. I could tell she was trying to figure out if I was just ugly or out of focus, so I took off the mask. Helen had her ratty silver hair pushed up under a ski cap, and was wearing what most men wear when they play golf.

I asked her why she wasn't down at one of the missions. "Don't like them." She loosened up a little and told me she often slept here and she always slept outside. She didn't like the people who ran the missions. She had been evicted from every charitable shelter as an incorrigible. "But, Princess," she said, "It doesn't matter." She loved her life. She praised the Lord. We praised the Lord together—shocking, I know!

She was everything that was good. I knew that in an instant. One of God's Trusting Angels, something I could never be. I felt her changing my life. I gave her my cart with all the booty I had collected from the free box, plus all the money I had in my pockets. She loved the pillow. I grabbed my bag, threw my mask in it and walked on down South of Market, sulking and angry.

How can this poor woman be living on the streets while the new Politically Correct Machine plays out corporate morality dramas pretending they are on the side of the good? My brain was on fire.

I got to Howard Street and bumped into the Marquee. He had a joint behind his ear. We smoked. I told him about Helen and how this was the future for many of us. He said, "Those Corpsuckers" a combination of "corporate," "corpse" and "suck." "Greed is the final great perversion—just think about it, Princess." They will never have enough.

The Marquee was a political critic. "I'll tell you something else, Princess, the Liberals and Conservatives are just as perverse. Everybody wants to be rich, that's all they care about. We live in a world where the powerful, the wealthy—on the left and the right—go to sleep in comfort, while innocents like Helen sleep in cold shadows and end up dying miserable deaths in fast food booths. I bet Her Mayorness is sleeping well tonight."

"Grant Junkies," We said together. "That Bitch. She and her Lizards should be sleeping in the streets." We acknowledged each other for our unique, depraved selves. I thanked him for the buzz, the hug, and the jive, we parted.

I thought about going to lower Mission under the freeway. Sometimes I would go there to sit and think in the dark, out of the rain. There are enough alleys down here for everybody. Perhaps I'd had enough ideological orgasms for one day.

I went to the Dutch Boy at 8th and Folsom to cruise instead. It was dead. Just desperate, funky irregulars drugged out in their cars. I crossed the street, climbed into my favorite refrigerator box, and went to sleep.

This charade went on for months. I could not get enough Monkey Man. I would be downtown, where no one even noticed my monkey face. Or I'd travel to the Haight to scare perfect clone boys fucking in Buena Vista bushes. "Some of these queens have no imagination," I'd laugh to myself.

Then one Saturday night I went to the Ambush, an arty darkside bar not far from home.

Wearing blacks, collar and leash, I transformed from bag woman to Master Bastard, ready to cavort in this M.C. Escher-esque, twisted landscape of levels and layers. My pet snake Tui was curled up in my leather jacket pocket where she loved to peek out into the night, just like her mistress!

I walked down the door ramp and stood next to the pinball machine until my eyes settled through the mask. I saw The Baron an actual member of a royal family from Belgium standing by the john. During the day he worked for the World Bank. But tonight he was reading a sign on the bathroom wall that said, "Neighbors have complained to the ABC (Alcohol and Beverage Control) about the pissing in the alley. The ABC then inspected the Ambush seven times and discovered: 1) cocksucking in the can, and 2) pot smoking with the help. The ABC can now suspend our beer and wine license and probably will." Someone had crossed out "will" and inserted "have." Thus, no beer tonight. I walked over and laid my leash on the bar. I ordered Calistoga water. Lou stuffed a lemon twist into the bottle with his middle finger and winked. He had seen the mask earlier in the day at a private showing. I was shaking the cage and the leather animals were itchy. Soon, the Baron made a move. I saw his hand go for my leash. I yanked it clear and stung him with it. Get the fuck out of here, I growled. Lou chuckled.

The Baron turned quickly so no one would notice his rejection. He didn't know who I was but I knew him all too well and recognition would spoil my fun. I chuckled but he could handle it. I picked up my slushed water and sucked it down. I had to get out of there. It was too stuffy, too noisy. It was too early for bars. I put the bottle down, nodded to Lou. I headed for my favorite inner sanctum where it was never too early, the 5th Street Glory Holes.

At the front door was the always radiant Irish lad Fuck Me Patty. He would let me in for free. I would need more drugs. I walked back to Isis—how forgetful of me—but fortunately it was just a few blocks and didn't take long. Now I could smoke going down through the Folsom.

I took the mask off and walked past The Stud, where Egg and Ms. Maroon were dancing in the street in full oblivion. They waved as I dashed. A few more feet down was the oldest leather bar South of Market, Febe's, on the corner of 11th. Motorcycles were lined up outside, just as the big buck daddies were inside. I quickened my pace. The Bolt, a working man's bar, was two more blocks down. I looked ahead to make sure the traffic was safe. At night, these bars shone as beacons making it possible to traverse the cobblestone meat rack in one piece.

I hungered for danger that lurked in the night but I appreciated the comfort of the familiar creatures cruising the sex establishments. I walked to Ringold Alley where late night cruising in the shadows was the sport of warriors who, like lusty nightcrawlers, come out from their holes into the darkened space.

I have spent hundreds of nights here in the cold rain looking for a warm interlude. I finished my joint in front of the old Red Star Saloon a few more blocks down. It had been gutted by the fire in The Barracks upstairs. I threw my roach in, to honor the resident divas. In another time this landmark of eroticism would have been a temple to male rites. Now it was only sweet memories. Yet, such juicy memories …!

The rest of the walk was the most dangerous. It was very dark. There were no more bars or baths, unless you count the bisexual Sutro-Baths as a real place. It was always too quiet and creepy through here. Maybe this is where I will become a vampire, I wondered? I clung to the storefronts, hiding in shadows of doorways as I made my way. I kept a brass flute in my jacket sleeve. With one strike, I'd bust your face. I got to 5th and turned left up past the abandoned lot and hotel. I walked crisscross, across to the private men's club, South of The Slot. Someone had moved the scorched glory hole booths from The Barracks third floor orgy room into this new storefront and balcony. It smelt like fire.

The Barrack's had burned mysteriously one balmy evening. Did we cry? It was like losing my family home. Lots of guys were coming by, taking away pieces of the building. I have a piece of a mural from the cowboy suite. Ruby Zebra told me he saw some leather guys dragging the glory holes out booth by booth. It didn't take me long to discover they had put them on the balcony in this new club.

I have a special attachment to these well-used walls. I recognized the Truly Gay graffiti about an old-timer we named Sniff that I had made him write. I thanked the Gods for saving, if only in a small way, this remnant from The Barracks, the hottest baths of my last millennium!

Looking back over my shoulder to see if I was being followed, I put Monkey Man on, and stepped over homeless winos on the walk. The Salvation Army Mission was right next door. I opened the black-painted door and announced, "Patty, it's me: The Princess."

"What the Fuck, Gurlll? What are you doing? Get your sick ass in here! Did the missionaries see you? Where'd you get that thing? Don't scare the old-timer, You Pig!"

I slipped into the red-lit darkness. Ahhhhh. The aroma of smoke, nitrates, and sweat in the shadows and in the pounding sounds of familiar cubicles.

Ninety-plus individual and double-sized mazed units designed specifically to suck dick. Half a dozen were exposed to the balcony overhead for voyeurs, or for drug and cum breaks. Other cubicles were totally darkened so you wouldn't have to see who, or what, did you. I entered a double that was fully, but dimly lit. It was under the bleachers with four glory holes. I locked the door and stood there waiting for hungry faces to appear.

Warrior holes in the walls. Mouths agape. Hungry tongues darting, slurping for my leash feast. Leather slapped against hot cavernous mouths, rubbing them with black, Big Mac denim ass. I used my dirty, sweaty hands to thumb-fuck their hungry faces. I would not let them have me. I would not respond to their faggot pleas to suck dick. Instead, I beat them with my covered cock. I wanted to tempt their lust, excite someone into action. "Beg to be fed, you fucking cock suckers …!"

Then, an explosion: SLAM! BANG! CRASH! WHOOSH—and the door to my booth was forced and flung open. I could hear the broken lock fall on the sticky stained floor. I turned as the brute entered, a large man looking intent and swarthy. I had seen him watching me from above. This was good!

He grabbed my leash and dragged me down to the corner of the booth. My kind of man! I needed this.

He said, "You're going to suck my cock, you fucking animal," straight into my monkey face. "Yes, Sir." I went down on my knees with a thud. He ripped open his studded pouch. Forcing me to eat at the trough of David, The God Priapus demanded satisfaction. The smell of testosterone filled my pores, saturating me. Pure Masculinity. A Combat of the Gods.

Fucking my face, he uncovered my desire. Pounding my head off his bones he came, ripping off my Monkey Man mask like a large shredded condom. He left instantly, leaving me unmasked on the floor, a pathetic shining mess. Dragging my act up, I made my way home through the dark to Isis, satiated, filthy, and sublimely relaxed.

I slipped Tui, the yellow striped garter snake, back into her pool where she perched her head on her gardenia. I chalked up one more mark on the headboard. My sweetheart, so-called lover, who I hadn't seen in weeks, wanted me to keep track of all the men I had sexual encounters with. He felt I was obsessed with men. I thought, "Yeah. Just another cookie from the jar to dream on, Princess." And I went to sleep.

Soon our new dreams would turn into new nightmares. The sexcapades of the seventies would meet head on with a covert viral infestation from cosmic and political enemies.

Soon, death would be everywhere.

Lee Mentley, July 28, 2012. Photo by Daniel Nicoletta

AFTERWARD

Accepting reality has made me miserable,
grumpy and a real S.O.B..
I accept that as the cost of integrity.

I do not think of myself as a writer but a story teller who is more comfortable on stage than on paper. Compatriots say my stories are fun in a dark way, reminiscent of William Boroughs perhaps, but I see them closer to Christopher Isherwood's Berlin stories, particularly those about Sally Bowles. In Cabaret, a fun-loving community is busy being entertained by a Master of Ceremonies at a local bistro. He presents all they could want to see onstage. Offstage, however, someone is turning his neighbors into the Gestapo for his own profit, while he simultaneously seeks recognition as a faux hero.

In The Castro of today 2015 the legacy of Harvey Milk has turned into "Profit Over The Rainbow."

On Christmas Eve 2013, the San Francisco Homeless Youth Alliance was shut down. I know where Harvey Milk would have been that night: right out in front with his baseball bat.

Where were the so-called Gay Leaders and elected officials of San Francisco circa 2013? No doubt feasting behind their White Picket Fences!

Fame Maggots who normally can't be pulled away from microphones were nowhere to be found because Harvey wasn't there and no money was to be made, only work to be done.

Heads of gay organizations, making six-figure vulture salaries, living off death and fear would not open their doors to these desperate kids seeking sanctuary. Nor have they defended people with HIV/AIDS, the elderly or poor Gays who have been evicted from their homes for further Gay profit. No. These Fame Maggots are busy applauding themselves for cleaning up The Castro by removing benches so no one can sit, and making it illegal for gay homeless youth to be caught standing and/or sitting too long in The Castro. Nudists, street musicians, and citizens wanting to relax at Milk Plaza, paid for with their tax dollars, are now refused respite in their own community. Nudists, who came to San Francisco in the 1970s, where being nude in public was made legal in a hard fought legal battle are now harassed, arrested and bankrupted in court. Gay Inc. vultures who have corporate sponsors and government grants are now silent over merchants who have seized control of our Rainbow Flag which has been forbidden use by certain groups like the Transgendered.

While the Gayourgeoisie are busy decimating our community, tourists are walking on the rainbow in the crosswalks for profit, these money grubbers refuse to see that the Right Wing has tightened a noose around our necks. From U.S. senators to religious leaders of all stripes, we have Kill-The-Gay campaigns spreading across the country and around the world resulting in draconian laws, beatings and murders. This includes people being thrown from buildings in The Middle East to being burned alive in Uganda, bringing the very definition of "Faggot" back from the vault of medieval religious insanity. These White Picket Fencers feel safe behind money and corporate storefronts, imagining when the Right Wing Christian Terrorists take complete control of all three branches of government they will somehow be safe in their Gay Potemkin Village.

Echoing Anita Bryant's campaign, the Gay Right Wing is expressing concern about their children seeing Sexual Outlaws on the streets—streets we had made safe in The Sexual Revolution that created this village. Who will be the next target? The divine decadence of a man in a dress, a Cockette, Sisters of Perpetual Indulgence, and The Emperor's Court, or a Drag King?

I wonder if people who now worship Harvey Milk understand what their Saint would do?

Harvey Milk would kick their Mother Fucking Asses!

REAL ESTATE SPECULATION CAUSES CANCER...

in our neighborhood. The tourist trade is taking over desperately needed moderate-income housing and neighborhood serving businesses.

The building on the South-west corner of 19th and Castro was recently taken over by Herth Realty and its henchpersons Joe Chavez and Boyd Swartz. They have sent notices of termination to all of the people living there and to the corner grocery and two antique stores. They plan on turning the property - and the rest of 19th Street between Castro and Collingwood - into high-turnover-high density commercial uses. Including changing 2nd floor flats into commercial uses.

Eureka Valley needs to retain its already over-pressured housing stock. We need to keep neighborhood businesses who serve our residents. We dont need to become another Union Street.

At its meeting on November 15 the Eureka Valley Promotion Association authorized the picketing of Herth Realty and Mssrs. Chavez and Swartz. The San Francisco Tenants Union has joined in our activities as has the San Francisco Housing Coalition. We are united in our opposition to speculation with people's housing and livelihood.

The new owners gave the current tenants a grand total of 30 days to get out. What a Christmas present! One of the tenants is a 95-year old blind, crippled woman who has lived there 20 years. Three other flats have had their tenants already removed by these "entrepreneurs." The grocery store has been there 15 years under the same ownership. Previously there has been a grocery store for the past 90 years. The two antique stores have been around providing moderately priced furniture 6 and 10 years.

It's time for Eureka Valley residents to come out of the closet against housing speculation and against eviction of neighborhood businesses. Rent increases of 400% are unacceptable. We will not tolerate this any longer.

If you share our concerns, call Herth Realty at 861-5200 and let them know how you feel. Let Herth, let Chavez, let Swartz know that the businesses that move in will not be patronized. Join us.

Lee Mentley, President-elect, Eureka Valley Promotion Assn
Sue Hestor, Past-president, Eureka Valley Promotion Assn
Frank Fitch, President, Eureka Valley Promotion Assn
Anne Dewsbury, San Francisco Tenants' Union
and dozens of others

Flyer by Lee Mentley, circa 1975

HRH'S HULA PALACE GAY GLOSSARY

590 Castro: A large top floor flat on the corner of Castro and 19th Streets North West. Site of the original series of Hula Palace Salons dated from December 1973 to October 1976.

A.

Adrian Craig, 1. Hula Palace artist. 2. Producer of New Wave groups, Tuxedomoon, Winston Tong, 1980 "Off The Wall" tour of the East Coast Mud Club, Max's and the legendary Noh Mercy tour to Madame Wong's in Los Angeles. 3. Editor of Eureka Noe Valley Artist Coalition or ENVAC newsletter at Top Floor Gallery. 4. Performance artist.

Angels of Light, An offshoot from the Cockettes created by George Harris aka "Hibiscus," an underground performer of immense presence in the world of make believe and glamour along with other Cockettes who wanted to do free shows. Shows included Holy Cow, Paris Sights Under The Bourgeoisie Sea, and Myth Thing among many others.

Artista aka The Goddess Artista, 1. Remarkable golden haired personage in leather gowns belted by a large black leather studded with the word GODDESS, . 2. Multimedia artist. 3. Resident Diva at Hamburger Mary's. 4. Bouncer at The Stud. 5. Exhibited at Hula Palace Salons, Top Floor Gallery, The Stud, The Ambush, Hamburger Mary's, Fey Way and The Barracks. 5. Lived at 14 Isis Street #5, South of Market, San Francisco.

B.

Barracks, 1. A notorious Victorian hotel turned into a raunchy three story bath house of willful ill repute, drugs and extreme sexual theater. 2. On the first floor was the Red Star Saloon. 3. Torched in 1981. 4. One time home of Jesus Christ Satan the Crown Prince Arcadia.

Black Mountain, 1. Founded in 1933 by John Andrew Rice, Theodore Dreier, and other former faculty members of Rollins College, Black Mountain was experimental by nature and committed to an interdisciplinary approach, attracting a faculty that included many of America's leading visual artists, composers, poets, and designers, such as musician John Cage, Buckminster Fuller, who invented the geodesic dome. 2. Artists from Black Mountain who exhibited at Top Floor Gallery include, Robert Duncan, William McNeil, Kanute Styles, Mary Bowles, Etta Dickmann, Ruth Asawa, Tom Field, Robert De Niro Sr. and Caldwell Brewer.

Bunny Honey, 1. John Warren of Nantucket. 2. Ms. Janitress of Hamburger Mary's 3. Sunshine Johnny 4. Six feet three inches of deeply tanned sweetly divine flesh.

C.

Cockettes, 1. Extraordinarily flamboyant ensemble of unusual humans costumed in gender/species defying drag with tons of glitter and cardboard living in a paradise of the mind. 2. They created legendary midnight musicals at the Palace Theater in North Beach. With titles such as Tinsel Tarts in a Hot Coma, Pearls over Shanghai, Hot Greeks, and films Tricia's Wedding and Elevator Girls in Bondage. These all singing, all dancing extravaganzas featured elaborate costumes, rebellious sexuality, and exuberant chaos. 3. It was once said by Disco Diva Sylvester "If you are walking down the street and see a bunch of people having fun in a mud puddle, that's the Cockettes." 4. Many Cockettes and Angels of Light performed and shared other art forms at the Hula Palace salons. There are too many names to list them all, but the short list would include Pristine Condition, Dolores Deluce, Viva, Sister Ed Luckin, Martin Worman, Brent Jensen, Steven Arnold, Sebastian, Toots Taraval aka Teddy Kern, Rumi Missabu, Wally Cockette, Goldie Glitters, John Flowers, Bobby Burnside, Ralph Sauer, Janice Sukitis, Kreemah Ritz, Sweet Pam Tent, Scrumbly Koldewyn, John Rothermel, Dusty Dawn, Ocean Michael Moon, Fayette Hauser, Esmeralda, Lendon Sadler, and the magnificent Tahara plus many more.

D.

Danny Nicoletta, 1. Danny started his photographic career in 1975 as an intern to Crawford Barton, another exhibitor at the Hula Palace, who was then a staff photographer for the national gay magazine, The Advocate. 2. In 1974, when he was 19, Nicoletta first met Harvey Milk and Scott Smith at Castro Camera and took many now well-known photographs of Milk. One of his iconic photos of Harvey has become a U.S. Postage Stamp. 3. In the feature film Milk, a biographical film based on the life of Harvey Milk directed by Gus Van Sant. Daniel Nicoletta is played by Lucas Grabeel.– Nicoletta himself plays Carl Carlson and served as the still photographer on the film. 4. Nicoletta was one of the founders of the San Francisco International GLBTQ Film Festival, now known as the Frameline Film Festival.. 5. Danny had his first public exhibit at the Hula Palace Salon.

Dianne Feinstein, 1. Became Mayor of San Francisco after the assassinations of Mayor George Moscone and Supervisor Harvey Milk in 1978. 2. U.S. Senator. 3. Power and Money is her first language. 4. War Criminal.

Divine, 1. Born Harris Glenn Milstead, also known by his stage name as Divine (October 19, 1945 – March 7, 1988), was an American actor, singer and drag queen. A close collaborator with independent filmmaker John Waters, he was a character actor, usually performing female roles in cinematic and theatrical appearances, and adopted a female drag persona for his music career; People magazine described him as the "Drag Queen of the Century."

F.

Flush, something we said every time we saw a lizard or maggot.

Mz. Forrest Lawn. 1. Actor. 2. Married well. 3. Lover of dogs. 4. Sheila Doyle

G.

Gayourgeoisie, 1. The Homosexual Bourgeoisie 2. Queens who would still be in the closet if it wasn't for the Truly Gay. 3. The Gay 1%.

Gay, 1. Possessing or manifesting a free and generous spirit. 2. Fabulous. 3. Not interested in convention.

Gurl, Gurrll, Gurrrllll,Grrr 1. A silly boy or boys, 2. A serious boy or boys being silly. 3. An extremely butch sister may be called Grrr.

Truly Gay, 1. Queers before Anita Bryant and the national politically correct movement. 2. When Gay did not mean your sexuality but your awesome spirit, as in many of the Cockettes and Angels of Light were heterosexual, bi-sexual, or of dubious sexuality but they were all Truly Gay. 3. A reader of beads. 4. The Drag Queen Lulu.

H.

Harvey Milk's Campaign Speech at 330 Grove Gay Pride Center: The Hope Speech: http://voiceofdemocracy.umd.edu/milk-youve-got-to-have-hope-speech-text/

Hula Palace Salon, 1. A residence and gallery performance space based on natural timing through astrology with the I Ching, as defined by Carl Jung and Wilhelm Reich in their theory of Cosmo-biology. 2. A place to be entertained, enlightened and indulge your favorite mood elevators. 3. Performances and exhibits first occurred at 590 Castro Street from December 1973 to October 1976, then at Top Floor Gallery 330 Grove Street San Francisco, with a 25th Reunion Salon in April 1994 along with the 30th Anniversary of the Cockettes.

Salons @: The Hula Palace 590 Castro Street:

Winter Salon The Comet Kohoutek - December 21-23, 1973

Rite of Spring - January 25-27, 1974

Primavera March 20, 1974

The Golden Calf - May 17-19, 1974

Festival of Leaves June 21, 1974

Chen Arousing Thunder March 12-15, 1975

Tui, The Sorceress, October 1-5, 1975

The Gentle Wind– spring 1976 - salon dates unclear? Possibly March 19, 20 & 21.

A Fall Salon - 1976 - dates and name unclear? Possibly September 24, 25 & 26.

330 Grove:

The Horse Salon- February 7, to March 3, 1978

Les Enfants du Palais - April 1, 1979

Mission Street Salon:

Reunion Salon - The Joyous - April 1-3, 1994

HRH, 1. HIS OR HER ROYAL HIGHNESS
2. LEE MENTLEY

I.

Iory Allison, 1. A writer, dancer, photographer, interior designer and art collector. His books include The Family Jewels: Book One of the Glamour Galore Trilogy, The Mermaid and The Sailor, and Naughty Astronautess. 2. Iory was a curator, performer and exhibitor at Hula Palace Salons. 3. Iory retired to Boston to live with his lovely husband Leo Romero of Casa Romero, one of Boston's finest dining establishments.

J.

Jack Fritscher, Ph.D. An American author, novelist, magazine journalist, gay historian, photographer, videographer, university professor, and social activist known internationally for his fiction and non-fiction analyses of gay popular culture. As a pre-Stonewall gay activist, he was an out and founding member of the American Popular Cultural Association. Fritscher is the founding San Francisco editor-in-chief of Drummer Magazine.

Janice Roland aka Jano, 1. Artists' model. 2. Actor 3. Muse to master painters Demetrie Kabbaz and Wayne Quinn. 4. Philanthropist of the arts.

Jerry Taylor, 1. Hula Palace artist. 2. Top Floor Gallery associate. 3. Painter.

Jim Campbell, 1. Painter. 2. Coordinator of Life Drawing Sessions at Top Floor Gallery 330 Grove. 3. Set and costume design for Gallery Theatre Company, Noh Oratorio Society, The Cockettes, Les Nickelettes. 4. aka "The Marquee". 5. Hula Palace artist

Jimmy Coker, 1. Hula Palace artist. 2. Curator at Top Floor Gallery. 3. Executive Board Member of Pride Foundation. 4. Aka, my sister Ann.

John Serrian: 1. Artist in multiple mediums. 2. Hula Palace artist. 3. Producer Gallery Theatre Company. 4. Top Floor Gallery associate.

K.

Ken Dickmann, 1. Noted theatre and film critic and founding member of the international film festival named FILMX. 2. Gay activist in San Francisco during the 1970's. 3. Member of The Society for Individual Rights all male reviews of Broadway shows' in San Francisco like Little Mary Sunshine, Oklahoma, Dames at Sea. 4. Columnist for the San Francisco Sentinel under "Stepping Out with Ken Dickmann". 5. Theater critic for the Los Angeles Times. 6. Publicist for Rogers & Cowan and MGM.

L.

Lady Dianne, 1. Artist, dancer and wild woman from Hawaiian Islands via East LA. 2. Performed Medusa at Hula Palace Salon along with Iory Allison as a part of Lee Mentley's MFA degree.

HRH Lee Mentley, aka ELA, aka ELA Lee, aka The Princess, aka the author. ETC...,

Les Plush, 1. Vocalist, performer, astrologer and writer. 2. Created first Hula Palace Salon developing the idea of using I Ching symbols and astrology for salon themes and timing 3. Winner "Miss Peace Love" at Cockette Misdemeanor Pageant. 4. Aka, Linda Carne, Etta Linda, Erlinda, and just Etta. 5. Queen of brown rice, beans, lentils, cumin and curry.

Lizard People, 1 People who make their living off of hate, fear and death. 2. Those in search of power for power's sake. 3. Fake Liberals.

Lou Rudolph, 1. Hula Palace exhibitor, South of Market artist at The Ambush, Fey Wey, and Top Floor Gallery. 2. Known for his signature performance paintings of Punk Rock and New Wave musical artists live on stage. 3. A true sweetheart.

M.

Maggie Lind, 1. Neon Maroon, actress, stylist and general pain in the ass, this Real Girl is a knock out.

Maggots, 1. People who live off of hate and fear in association with Lizard People. 2. Fake humans. Blah, blah, blah.

Michael Shain: 1. Painter, writer, and performance artist. During the 70s he created the cabaret chanteuse Mona Mandrake. 2. Host of Men's Life Drawing Sessions at the Hula Palace and Top Floor Gallery. 3. Member of the Noh Oratorio Society.

Mink Stole, 1. Born Nancy Paine Stoll, better known by the stage name Mink Stole, is an American actress from Baltimore, Maryland. 2. Mink began her career working for director of Dreamlanders, John Waters. 3.Co-star of "Pink Flamingos" and many others. 4. Extraordinary human being.

P.

Paul Hardman, 1. In the 1970s and early 1980s, Mr. Hardman published the California Voice, a San Francisco gay newspaper. In 1984, he founded the Alexander Hamilton Post, the country's first American Legion post with a gay and lesbian focus, which played an active role in the national battle over gays and lesbians in the military. 2. Mr. Hardman served on the board of the Society for Individual Rights and the American Association for Personal Privacy. He was executive director of Pride Foundation and Pride Center at 330 Grove Street. 3. Served as president of the San Francisco Veterans Affairs Commission.

Pérez. 1. She was a core member of the Hula Palace, hostess at salons, photographer, journalist, and exhibitor. 2. Faculty member of the University of Hawai'i. 3. A freelance writer with a focus on cultural history and natural resources worldwide. 4. Associate editor for a publishing company in Honolulu. 5. Photojournalist 6. Breaker of hearts.

Politically Correct, 1. A movement on The Left to enslave language and dominate the world. 2. Aka, PC.

Pride Foundation, 1. The Pride Foundation was founded August 8, 1973 in San Francisco and operated by a board of directors. A partial list of the organization's founders includes Zane Thomas, B.J. Beckwith, George Mendenhall, Roberta Buba, Charlotte Coleman, John Wahl, Perry Wood, Larry Littlejohn, Jimmy Coker and Paul Hardman. Lee Mentley served on the board's executive committee. 2. The Foundation served the gay and lesbian community by providing direct legal assistance, especially in cases of discrimination and defamation, engaging in educational research, conducting classes, and providing assistance in social and health services. It provided services such as gay legal referrals, a senior citizens program, a gay tourist and visitor's information bureau, health referrals, a coalition to defend gays in the military, art classes, drop-in facilities for youth, job placement, and a social group for older men known as G40+. The Foundation also operated the Top Floor Gallery for local gay artists. 3. Beginning in 1976, Foundation Chairman Paul Hardman began requesting use of 330 Grove Street, which was under the ownership of the San Francisco Redevelopment Agency. A signed agreement of occupancy was negotiated between the Foundation and the Redevelopment Agency, and the Foundation began operating the Pride Center at 330 Grove, their gay and lesbian community services center, in December of that year. Pride Center served as the Foundation's offices and also provided low-cost meeting spaces for other neighborhood organizations. Due to disputes over-funding and occupancy of 330 Grove, Hardman, who had been president and chairman since the organization's founding, was pressured to resign in 1979, increasing internal conflicts in the Foundation's board instigated by Mayor Dianne Feinstein. Although this mayor had promised the board they would receive the purposed funding if they forced Hardman out and left the 330 Grove building yet it took thirty years for a new center to open. 4. Pride Foundation papers on file at ONE Archives, Los Angeles, California

Q.

Quaaludes, 1. Quaaludes were the most popular brand of a medical drug called methaqualone. Healthcare professionals prescribed it for a wide range of conditions, including sleeplessness and anxiety. Recreational users began experimenting with it, and "ludes" quickly became an equally popular non-medical drug in many countries. It was eventually declared illegal in many countries because of its addictiveness and its association with crime. 2. Recreational buyers adopted various codenames for Quaaludes, including ludes, quads, soaps, Disco Bisquets and Lemmons. One of the most popular slang names was "714," which was based on the identifying numbers etched into each pill by the manufacturer. 3. This drug depresses the body's central nervous system, primarily its brain activity. It relaxes inhibitions for five to eight hours on a single normal dose. Some people also have more unusual side effects, including increased sexual arousal and numbness of the extremities. 4. The 1970s saw a surging popularity of Quaaludes being used in social settings like dance clubs. Many people deliberately ingested them with alcohol, and other drugs, these combinations sometimes caused memory "blackouts," with people reporting no recollection of events that occurred during their intoxication.

R.

Rainbow Flag, 1. Created by over 100 artists from Eureka Noe Valley Artist Coalition and community volunteers at Top Floor Gallery with funding from the Hotel Fund through The Pride Foundation. Original concept of Lynn Segerblom, aka Mz. Argyle Rainbow Fairie who was the professional rainbow artist for Capizo. 2. No, Gilbert Baker was not Betsy Ross. He was just one of the artists who worked on the flags as co-chair of the Gay Day Parade decorating committee along with Ms. Lynn Segerblom and many others.

RG's, 1. Real Girls.

Robert Kirk 1. aka Cirby, 2. Actor, model. 3. Erotic Illustrator of Leather and S&M erotica under the name Cirby. 4. One of the original roommates at 590 Castro Street Hula Palace 5. Rodeo Cowboy and bartender at The Midnight Sun. 6. Exhibitor at Fey Wey Gallery.

Robert Opel, 1. A photographer and art gallery owner, most famous as the man who streaked the 46th Academy Awards in 1974. 2. In March 1978, Opel opened Fey-Way Studios, a gallery of gay male art, at 1287 Howard Street in San Francisco The gallery helped bring such erotic gay artists as Tom of Finland and Robert Mapplethorpe and Camille O`Grady to national attention. Opel was murdered on the night of July 7, 1979, during a robbery of the studio by Robert E. Kelly and Maurice Keenan. 3. Many believe this murder was politically motivated because his expose drama 'The Execution of Dan White' would draw attention to the people Robert believed were behind the Moscone and Milk assassinations.

Robert Oppel, 1. Artist Robert Opel's nephew who created a film on his uncle's murder entitled "Uncle Bob". 2. Artist, film maker, musician. 3. Humanitarian. 4. A total sweetheart.

Ruth Weiss: 1. World renowned poet of the Beat Generation who gave special readings at Hula Palace Salons. 2. Herb Cane saluted her as 'Goddess of The Beats.' 3. Performed with the illusive Mona Mandrake on immaculate occasions. 4. Performed in several films by Steven Arnold. 5. Artist's model to Black Mountain artists.

S.

Shauna Snowflake, 1. Flamingo dancer. 2. Mother of two brilliant young men. 3. World Traveler.

Scotty Smith, 1. A gay rights activist best known for his romantic relationship with Harvey Milk. Smith was instrumental to Milk's career as an activist and politician. He organized and managed Milk's campaigns for public office from 1974 to 1977 and his influence was widely in evidence after Milk was elected to the San Francisco Board of Supervisors in 1977. 2. Smith was well known for orchestrating the Coors beer boycott and putting Milk at the forefront of the issue, creating one of the first public displays of power by the gay community.

Same Sex Marriage Case in The Castro, 1970's.
In this excerpt from the Independent Lens documentary Limited Partnership, Filipino American Richard Adams and Australian Tony Sullivan talk about how they first met and fell in love in the early 1970s in Los Angeles, and how immigration laws at the time gave them no rights as a gay couple. They were men without a country.

http://video.pbs.org/video/2365483477/

T.

Top Floor Gallery, 1. Gay artist, gallery and performance space funded by San Francisco Arts Commission N.A.P., The Pride Foundation, The Hula Palace and The Eureka Noe Valley Artists Coalition. 2. Located at 330 Grove Street Pride Center. 3. Where the Rainbow Flag was created by over 100 artists. 4. Operated the overnight suicide prevention hot lines. 5. Provided overnight shelter for Gay homeless youth.

W.

White Picket Fences, 1. Homosexual pretenders who want to be normal 2. Wants to control people. 3. Strive to be controlled. 4. Loved the 1920s, gilded greed. 5. Gayourgeoisie 5. The Gay One Percent.

Wart, aka Walter Caplan. 1. The District of Columbia Court of Appeals. IN RE: Walter H. CAPLAN, Respondent. No. 96-BG-541. —March 27, 1997—Before FERREN, FARRELL, and RUIZ, Associate Judges, Following his conviction and sentence in the Superior Court of the State of California, County of San Francisco, for grand theft (§ 487 of the California Penal Code) and practice of law without a license (§ 6126(b) of the California Business and Professions Code), respondent was disbarred from the practice of law by the Supreme Court of the State of California. The Board on Professional Responsibility likewise recommends disbarment, see D.C.Code § 11-2503(a) (1995), on the ground that the theft statute under which respondent was convicted involves moral turpitude per se. See In re Colson, 412 A.2d 1160, 1168 (D.C.1979) (en banc). We agree with that conclusion and accept the Board's recommendation. Criminal offenses involving theft and fraud inherently involve moral turpitude. In re Sluys, 632 A.2d 734 (D.C.1993); In re Slater, 627 A.2d 508 (D.C.1993); In re Schwartz, 619 A.2d 39 (D.C.1993); In re Boyd, 593 A.2d 183 (D.C.1991). The crime of grand theft under California law, requiring as it does a felonious intent to steal or take property in addition to the actual stealing or taking, e.g., People v. Arriola, 330 P.2d 683, 164 Cal. App.2d 430 (1958), inherently involves moral turpitude.

http://caselaw.findlaw.com/dc-court-of-appeals/1120108.html

Addendum #1

The Term Allegedly: I repeat; these stories allegedly happened in the 1970's while I was watching them play out. They may or may not have happened exactly the way I experienced them on sex, drugs & Disco.

Addendum #2

Betrayal:

This is the thing I hate most in life.

I know people who are very good at betrayal.

I have a list of those who have betrayed artists.

Ripping off art under the guise of supporting the arts is betrayal of the worst kind.

No one has a right to walk away with an artist's work without permission

If you witness this, expose them.

I have a list of these malefactors.

And I practice what I preach!

Addendum #3

A Recollection on Robert Opel From Camille O`Grady ..., I was in LA when it happened, as I was performing there, though I was living in and very politically active in SF.., Robert Opel, who was also assassinated that year, possibly for his own actions, jumped on a plane when we heard about that ridiculous decision! I feared for his life at the time, already. San Francisco was definitely a battleground at the time. I remember coming up with a crack about 'the meek inheriting the earth re: the Chinese who were on their way to becoming the world power they are today by quietly taking on all of that trade and manufacturing that the US. was passing on to them...however, I was, like everyone else I knew, furious about the final verdict and sentencing. In the Pride parade that year, we put on a performance piece in which Robert Opel (in full leather)'shot' a friend who was a ringer for White, and wearing a white jumpsuit. We rigged him to 'bleed' and after my band and I performed on our parade float, the action was done as we neared City Hall. Though we had gone through all of the proper channels to get 'permission' to do the piece, we got threatening calls about it. It went off perfectly, and it was so successful, it made the entire (network) news programs at the time, the question being asked was, 'What if I, a gay leather man shot Dan White? What kind of sentence would I get?' Robert was murdered and I escaped with my own life only a week or so later, on July 9, 1979.

Addendum #4

I'm sorry if I did not mention you or anyone you would have wanted in the book. Please get a pen and write yourself in.

_____

_____

HRH Dowager Princess visits the Hula Palace, 2012.
Photo by Daniel Nicoletta

TIME AS A UNIFYING THEME AT THE HULA PALACE SALONS

By Les Plush

*I*t could be one of the most ancient and original concepts in human culture, that as we move through time we are influenced by it. Inclinations, perceptions and thoughts—impulses—are infused with the currents of the moment, and creativity and expression carry with them the vital pulse of the time of their inception and delivery. As in quantum theory, we are both in and of the flow of time.

A word comes to mind—"conspire"—which literally means to breathe together. We absorb the present as breath as we inhale and exhale each moment. Coincidentally, the literal meaning of the word "Aloha" is the sharing of the breath of life.

The Salons were developed as we of the Hula Palace conspired to fashion events that considered the current creative efforts of our community. The use of seasonal themes from the I Ching provided a flexible motif for bringing to expression creative work in performance and visual arts.

Themes for the Salons were inspired by a seasonal diagram of eight symbols or Trigrams called the Inner World Arrangement. This comes from the body of thought associated with the I Ching and Taoism in which the primal forces of Ying and Yang interact. The concept of each trigram, which is based on a force of nature, is accessible and open for interpretation. For the Inner World Arrangement has to do with inner or subjective awareness of cyclic flow, currents of the inner life.

With my music partner Terry Ludwar who played wind instruments, nights of performances were opened with sung versus inspired by the concurrent trigram. Other performers and artists were free to express their work. Some were aware of the themes and many may not have been. For in a way it did not matter; time with myriad streams flows through each of us as exhale and inhale together at The Hula Palace.

The first Salon commenced on December 21st of 1973. It was simply called Winter Salon. This is the point in the year when light and the force of the Yang principle again begin to increase. In the Inner World Arrangement the symbol is K'an, the force of water flowing through an abyss. The symbol is made up of two yin lines, symbolic of earth and receptivity, with a yang line, representing heaven and creativity, in the center position. The spirit at this point of the year is encased in the material and must increase before it can flow over each new barrier or limitation. The Yang principle contained within this stream molds to the shape of the abyss in order to pass through it. Nothing will stop the power of the spirit and at Winter Solstice, with the increasing light of the Heavens, the spirit is renewed like a spring pouring out of the ground.

Hula Palace flyer by Jim Campbell

For that first night of the first Salon on the longest night of the year, I wrote verses starting with the line: "My arms are like limbs turning to the Sun, believe it's coming back, believe it's coming back."

For subsequent Salons I continued with a subjectively creative approach in performance and for developing themes for the Salons, using imagery that felt linked to the current trigram and the times that we were passing through. In later Salons information about the timing and themes was displayed along with the current astrological influences.

A Taoist principle expressed over and over again in the I Ching is that in order to influence others one must be able to take in what they are expressing of themselves. Let it react in you in a non-critical manner and only after that can one reach an exchange of perspective—of ideas.

The use of seasonal motifs then has the advantage of allowing for a wide range of subjective interpretation and creative freedom while discreetly promoting a unity through the common experience of the contemporary. The Hula Palace Salons set out in a rare accepting fashion to foster the growth of artistic work within a community. Still our doors remain open to the times and to the moment.

© 2006 Les Plush

The author has studied and worked in astrology and the I Ching for more than 40 years.

Made in the USA
Las Vegas, NV
28 January 2021